ACKNOWLEDGEMENTS

With thanks to

Vivien Lavis-Jones

for the photograph of the

Ringmore Church

and

The Church of Jesus Christ of Latter-Day Saints

for the permission to reproduce the IGI Microfiche.

This Edition Published By Grange Books
An Imprint of Grange Books PLC
The Grange
Grange Yard
London SE1 3AG

ISBN 1-85627-928-6

Tracking Ancestors

A Beginner's Guide

Anne Lavers

To

BILL

and

Miles, Marcus, Claire, Peter and Rory

CONTENTS

ABBREVIATIONS USED IN TEXT

AGRA	Association of Genealogists and Record Agents
BDM	Births, deaths, and marriages
BTs	Bishop's Transcripts
CoE	Church of England
CRO	County Record Office
FHS	Family History Society
FTM	Family Tree Magazine
GOONS	Guild of One-Name Studies
GRD	Genealogical Research Directory
GRO	General Register Office (In England: St. Catherine's House London)
HMSO	Her Majesty's Stationery Office
IGI	International Genealogical Index
IRC	International Reply Coupon (from Post Office)
LDS	Church of Jesus Christ of Latter-Day Saints
MI	Monumental Inscriptions
NGD	National Genealogical Directory
PCC	Prerogative Court of Canterbury
PCY	Prerogative Court of York
PPR	Principal Probate Registry (In England: Somerset House London)
PRO	Public Record Office (In England: Chancery Lane and Kew London)
RO	Record Office
SAE	Stamped, Self Addressed Envelope
SAG	Society of Australian Genealogists
SAGHS	South Australian Genealogy & Heraldry Society Inc.
SoG	Society of Genealogists, London
WDRO	West Devon Record Office

INTRODUCTION

This guide is for those who are new to the field of Family History. It is written by an enthusiastic researcher who has had many years experience in the tracing of ancestors, and who remembers the difficulties encountered, the help given graciously by others, and the joy of touching the first original document discovered. Then there has been that deep feeling of understanding, when an ancestor has been no longer just a name with a few dates attached, but has become a human being sharing with me, in another era, the ups and downs of life, in different yet often strangely similar ways. It is one's loss not to be able to converse and share thoughts with such an ancestor.

This is an open-ended, How-I-Got-Hooked book, the product of an experience that started as a leisurely hobby when I was given my father-in-law's notes on his family. It became a much more serious venture when I retired, and realised through a grandson's questions that he had missed out, due to the greater mobility within families in today's hectic world, on what I had taken for granted - the hearing of all the family legends when sitting on grandmother's knee, listening to tales of the past.

His ancestors and their offspring managed to live for long spells, on all five Continents. I have not managed to research them all, as yet but I have developed a flair for knowing where to look for help. That is what this guide is all about.

Acknowledgements:

Not all those who have given me of their time and knowledge can be mentioned here. However, I would like to thank Miss Marjory F. Jinkin of Plymouth, Devon, Mrs Nancy Baldock, AUA, FSAGHS, Honorary Librarian, Adelaide, and Dr M. D' Angelo of the University of Messina for their invaluable help and support over many years.

South Australia 1995.

Fictitious family Tree
of
John Wheeler Derby

figure 1

James Derby = Mary Dew
† by 1879

John Allen = Eliza (Batt?)

m: Easter 1879
Clarence Dew Derby = Eliza Batt Allen
* ca 1850 Sevenoaks?
† after 1908 before 1914

Eliza Batt Allen
* ca 1861 Turnbridge Wells
† ca 1918 London

William Fisher = Fanny

m: 24.5.1908, Sevenoaks
Clarence Allen Derby = Margaret Fisher

Clarence Allen Derby
called Bill
c 20.6.1879 St Saviours Southwark
† 23.11.1952, London
buried: St John's Wood

Margaret Fisher
* 2.4.1890
Sevenoaks
† 1.1.1972
buried: St John's Wood

John William Derby
* 10.10.1912, London
m: Josephine Wheeler 15.2.1942, Marylebone
† 12.11 1976, Abercorn Place, London
Buried: St John's Wood

John Wheeler Derby
* 1.1.1946, London
bap. 24.6.1946,
St Martin's in the Fields, Westminster
m: Elaine Roberts 15.3.1973
St Paul's Cathedral, London

HOW TO BEGIN

You need the following:

- 2 large pieces of paper.
- 1 soft pencil and a good eraser.
- 1 notebook, bound, for recording information on a date to date basis.
- 1 loose leaf folder, 1 sheet per ancestor and topic you wish to collate.

START WITH WHAT YOU KNOW YOURSELF

On the bottom centre of the first sheet, write your own name and below that the dates and places of your birth and marriage, and the name of your spouse.

Draw a short central line. Above this, write the name of your father, and then, underneath, the dates and places of his birth and marriage, the name of your mother, and the date of your father's death and burial should he no longer be alive.

Draw a short line in the centre upwards, finishing in an =. To the left of this, write the name of your paternal grandfather, and below this, the date and place of his birth, and, should he no longer be alive, the date and place of his death and burial. To the right of the =, write the same information about your paternal grandmother. Above the = write the date and place of their marriage.

Above your grandparents, write up in the same manner the details for their respective parents. (See Fig. 1, page 8)

On the bottom centre of the second sheet, write your own name and, below it, the dates and places of birth and marriage, and the name of your spouse. Above this, write the name of your mother. Then fill in the second sheet for your mother's family in exactly the same way as you filled in sheet one.

If you have completed this you know enough about genealogy to stop reading this chapter. However, the chances are that you have already encountered a number of stumbling blocks.

For instance, you may have discovered that your ancestor got married more than once, and you wonder how to record the facts.

My advice is to list your biological ancestor and write the details of the other spouse in your loose leaf notebook. (See fig 8, page 25)

Perhaps you don't know the information. Look at further topics in this volume:

- Consulting Relatives.

- Searching Indexes and the like.

- Births - Deaths - Marriages.

Once you have written up all you remember, there is one cardinal rule:

WORK BACK FROM WHAT YOU KNOW TO BE AN ABSOLUTE FACT AND TAKE NO SHORT CUTS.

To show just one of the many pitfalls, assume that a given ancestor has always been known as Bill Derby and you conclude that he was baptised William Derby. In actual fact, he was baptised Clarence Derby but hated that name, as well as his childhood name of Clarry, and changed it, at the first opportunity, to Bill Derby. You know his birthday and find, in a register of baptisms in the place where you think your ancestor was born, a William Derby listed at a suitable date. If you now follow the ancestral line of this William, you no longer research your own ancestors. With luck, you may later discover your error and also that William was a cousin of your ancestor, so that at least some of your data can be used.

Such things can happen more often than you might think. In the 19th century, there are numerous cases, where the same person was called, even in the family, by different names. In one case, the same person was referred to as Richard in some documents and as Henry in others. When both were researched, their dates and places matched, as well as the names of their spouses and children. So it was obvious there was only one man to whom all documents referred. Sometimes parents had several children of the same name. Generally, it is then found that the elder children had died before the births of the younger ones.

For this reason, it is recommended to go backwards step by step, starting with your own birth certificate. That gives the names of your parents and, being recent, includes your mother's maiden name. Then go to their marriage certificate, which at least in recent times, gives the maiden name of the bride and the age of both parties. As witnesses are often parents or relatives, this might give further clues which should be entered in the folder on the loose leaf relevant to the ancestor in question. So, by searching birth and marriage certificates alternatively, you might build up a direct line. It is absolutely essential to *note where the information was found* - for instance the Parish of the Birth Register, Volume, Folio number, where this register is kept, when it was consulted, and by whom. This might later save a great deal of time and effort, when conflicting evidence comes to light and it becomes essential to check and evaluate the data. You must remember that the information on certificates can never be better than the informant, at the time of registration.

Information confirmed by preferably 3 different sources (e.g. birthdate on birth certificate, marriage certificate and family Bible) can be written up on the sheet in ink.

CONSULTING RELATIVES

This is very helpful, particularly if they are elderly and have good memories. I gained the best results by visiting them alone. Few feel comfortable with a tape recorder present. The bound notebook is used here, with the date and the name of the relative interviewed as the page heading. The information noted previously is offered for inspection and comment. Special questions are prepared in advance.

Those fortunate to have several elderly relatives prepared to share information are likely to find not only that different memories are recalled, but also that firm statements made about past events , by different people, do not always correlate. This is one of the reasons why individual visits are preferable, although family gatherings do have the advantage of promoting discussions and jolting memories.

Whichever might be chosen as the best approach, family legend should never be adopted or discarded entirely without careful checking. Generally, it is found that legends have at least a grain of truth in them.

When going over the information collected in the bound notebook, transfer relevant items onto the sheets in the loose leaf folder with annotations like 'Aunt Jane'. Add the date of the conversation. Over the years, you learn if Aunt Jane's memory is more reliable than Aunt Mary's, and this insight might be a help in itself.

A lucky few will be given or allowed to copy old papers such as birthday books, which were very fashionable in Victorian days, family notes made by an ancestor, or an old family bible. These are treasures indeed.

Those who need more help and ideas on consulting family members might wish to read Eve McLauglin's Genealogical Guide, *Interviewing Elderly Relatives.*

DECIDING WHAT TO RESEARCH

This is a personal choice. It is often suggested that only one line at a time should be followed. This has the advantage

Loose Leaf Sheet from Note Book
for
CLARENCE ALLEN DERBY
known as BILL DERBY

(figure 2)

Birth Certificate found in St. Catherine's House.
Birth Index June quarter 1879, Reference: 1d 999

Christening: I.G.I. Greater London.
Bishop's Transcripts, Greater London Record Office
(self: 12.3.1986)

Marriage Certificate found in St. Catherine's House marriage
Marriage Index June quarter 1908, Reference: 2a 999
(in document folder)

Death Certificate obtained from St. Catherine's House. (In document folder)
Cemetery Burial Register and Headstone: See photographs. (In photo album)

Served in France 1914—1918. See Service Record obtained from
Ministry of Defence, Hayes, Middlesex. (In document folder)

Children:	William Fisher	12.9.1909 emigrated 1929 to USA.
	James	5.1.1911 † in France, February 1945
	John William	10.10.1912
	Eliza Margaret	4.4.1915 m: James Luscombe 1938
	Mary Elaine	30.10.1919 † 1921 from T.B.

Source: Family Bible

Aunt Lizzy (Luscombe), 23.12.1980: Remembers her father coming home on leave, just before the war was over and he was on crutches. He never returned to war. She and her father were sent out of London, to an uncle and aunt who lived in the country. Little Mary was sick and her mother went to hospital with her, so mother did not come. The boys also had to stay with mother, because they were already at school.

that one knows much of the information without having to check notes all the time and is of particular advantage if the family was in the same locality over many generations, so that the documents are in the same office or library.

Personally, I found that researching all the ancestral lines at the same time, and noting all the children I could find on their parent's individual sheets, helped me greatly, as there were many links between the various branches and I found documents of one branch whilst researching another. This method does require, however, much more organisation of notes.

STARTING THE SEARCH FOR DOCUMENTS

Before you buy a certificate, you need to know what to order. They are generally quite expensive and it is disappointing to find that you have bought an irrelevant document.

As genealogy has become an increasingly popular hobby, a great number of aids have become available. The majority of these are produced by enthusiastic volunteers who have grouped themselves into Family History Societies (FHS hereafter). Although there are a few older ones, such as the Society of Genealogists in London (SoG hereafter) which was founded in 1911, the majority are only in their second decade and new ones are forming. Most concentrate on their own area, county or State and produce three to four journals a year. They have formed a Federation of Family History Societies in England (FFHS hereafter) which has many overseas members. They exchange journals for their own libraries which can be very extensive. To become a member of such a society is of advantage and one can discuss one's problems. Most organise regular meetings, lectures and conferences. They generally have indexes, either printed, on microfilm or on microfiche, with the necessary readers, or know where they can be located. Groups go into local cemeteries, and copy from the gravestones all inscriptions, which are indexed by volunteers, and increasingly printed. All this costs money, which is often raised by asking for donations of varying amounts for consulting the indexes in response to postal enquiries.

Volunteers regularly index marriage registers, census returns and other records, and it is the work of the FFHS to coordinate the efforts of the various societies to prevent duplication of completed projects and those in progress. Members' Interest Lists are made available and often published, so that those who research the same name can establish contact.

All societies expect members to do their own research, as they rely largely - if not exclusively - on volunteers to assist, to the best of their ability, with advice on where else to look. There are books that can be borrowed and/or consulted on the spot, and most societies have a bookstall, where you may find many of the booklets mentioned here. Failing that, they are likely to know of the nearest specialist bookshop. You will find the addresses in the telephone book. Your nearest public library should also contain the latest edition of the Genealogical Research Directory (GRD hereafter) by Johnson & Sainty (described under 'Directories'). This, too, should have the addresses. An increasing number of societies provide help for members living afar. Non-members can write for help and are generally charged double the amount of the member's fee.

DIFFERENT DISPLAYS of the Family Tree

There are other generally accepted ways to display a family tree. One is simply to turn the information around by 90 degrees on an A4 sheet, so that the horizontal line gives the direct ancestral line and people of the same generation are one below the other.

Fictitious Family Tree
of
JOHN WHEELER DERBY
alternative version

figure 3

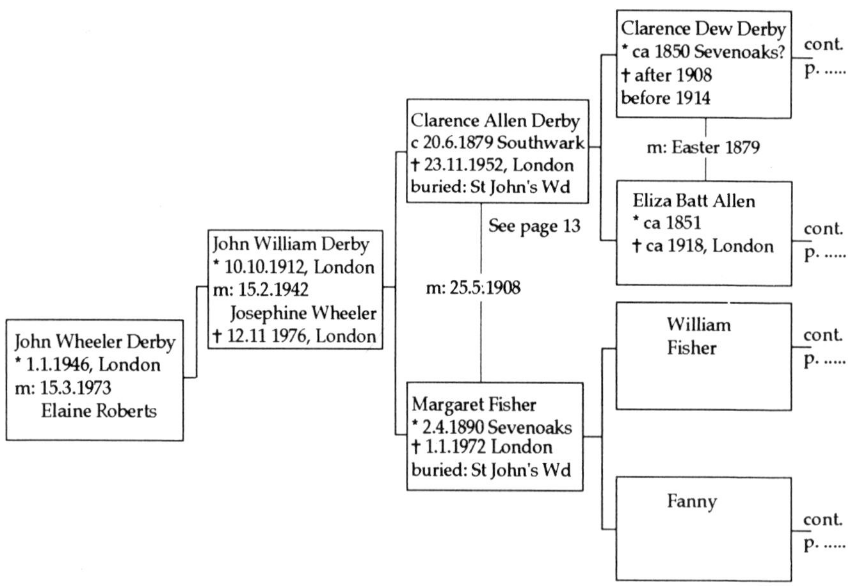

This is the form that I have chosen, because, although it takes me a long time to get the original layout on the computer, without any special programme except a word processing package, I can alter it as required. The Derby and Allen families would need to start new trees, on individual pages, taking great care to keep the same references for the same persons and indicating where else they can be found (e.g. number of page).

This allows me to print out sections of the tree for others, without also sending parts of trees which are not relevant to them.

The term 'Birthbrief' refers to a 'total descent'. In it, every direct ancestor, male and female, is traced, generally for no more than 5 generations, and all 16 great-great-grandparents are specified.

A birthbrief is sometimes used, by some societies, to enable members researching the same name to see quickly whether there are links between their individual investigations.

Birthbrief of John Wheeler Derby: Derby Wheeler, Fisher Good, Allen ..., Dew Batt?......

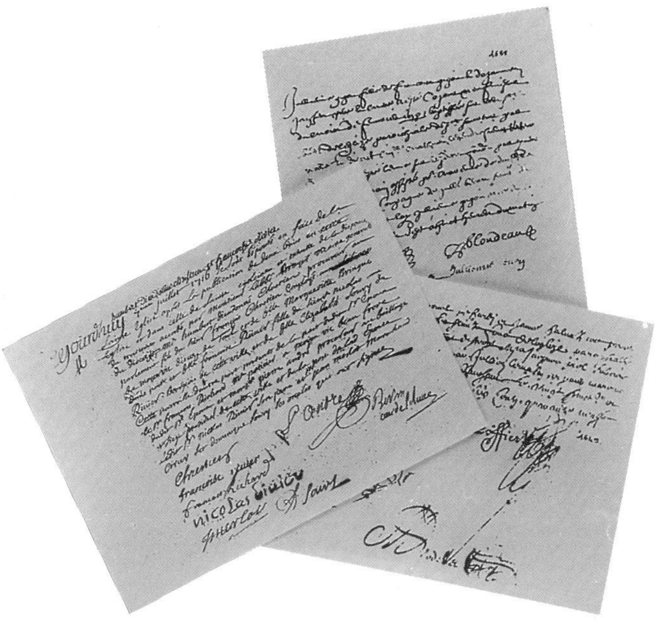

Fictitious Family Tree
of
JOHN WHEELER DERBY
alternative version
(ancestor numbered)

figure 4

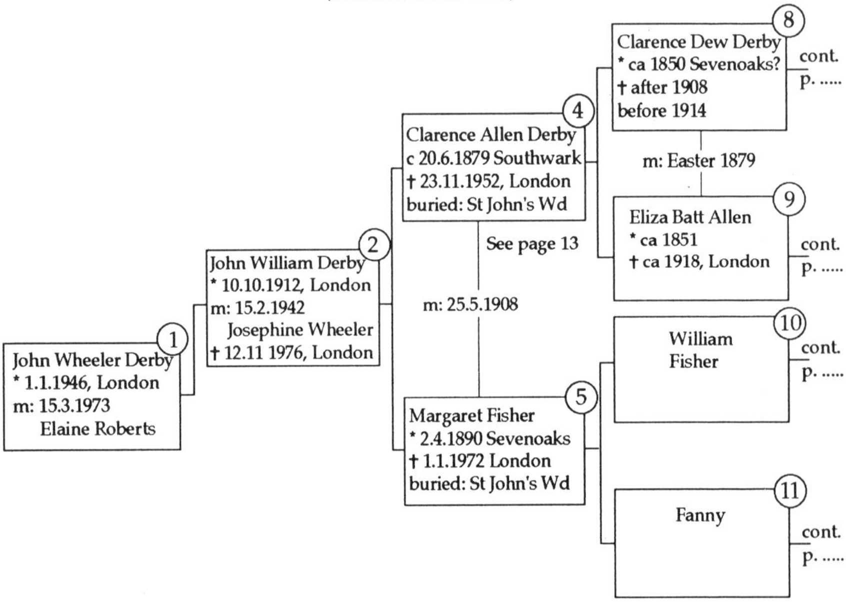

Numbers 3, 6 and 7, 12 to 15 are reserved for maternal ancestors.

This method works well for smaller families, particularly when there are no marriages between people on the tree elsewhere.

On the sheet of the individual, the eldest child of grandfather 4 can then be given the number 4-1 (assuming it is not the father number 2), and his eldest child 4-1-1. This would be a first cousin to oneself.

NUMBERING OF ANCESTORS

As more information is found, it becomes advisable to allot references to individuals. The simplest form is to number them. It is best to do this first in pencil, in order to allow for errors and for the possibility of changing one's mind about the method used.

A useful system begins with oneself as number 1, and continues in the following logical pattern: father 2, mother 3, paternal grandfather 4, paternal grandmother 5, maternal grandfather 6, maternal grandmother 7, father's paternal grandfather 8, etc.

If all known ancestors can be put thus onto one sheet, where all of the same generation are in a single vertical column, it can then be seen that the number given to the first ancestor of any particular generation; (i.e. the direct male line) is double the number of the preceding younger generation; i.e. father 2, grandfather 4, great-grandfather 8, great-great-grandfather 16 and so on.

CIRCULAR TREE

Another modified tree is the circular one. In the middle of the page, draw a small circle; write your initials within it, as it represents you. Draw a larger circle around it. Imagine it as a clock dial, and draw a line from the first circle through the second circle towards the edge of the page at 12 o'clock and at 6 o'clock. You now have two half circles. Write you father's name in the one between 12 o'clock and 6 o'clock, your mother's in the other. Draw an even larger circle and add a line at 3 and 9 o'clock. This results in the second ring having 4 sections. Between 12 and 3 o'clock, you write the name of your father's father, and, between 3 and 6, the name of his mother. Between 6 and 9 write your mother's father's name and, between 9 and 12 o'clock, your maternal grandmother's name. The next ring, cut again similarly, will give 8 sections for your great - grandparents, your paternal ancestors along the 12 o'clock line, with their spouses next.

You can extend this tree as much as you like. (See Fig. 5.)

It is important to remember that YOU choose which type of tree you wish to use. I suspect that this last form would be suitable for someone who knows all ancestors over several generations; for others, 'missing ancestors' would become all too obvious. One main advantage of this tree is that it can help the beginner to understand one way of numbering ancestors, using the generation grid.

The circular tree is of great advantage when trying to establish whether a given medical condition, such as asthma, is inherited in this family.

CIRCULAR TREE

(figure 5)

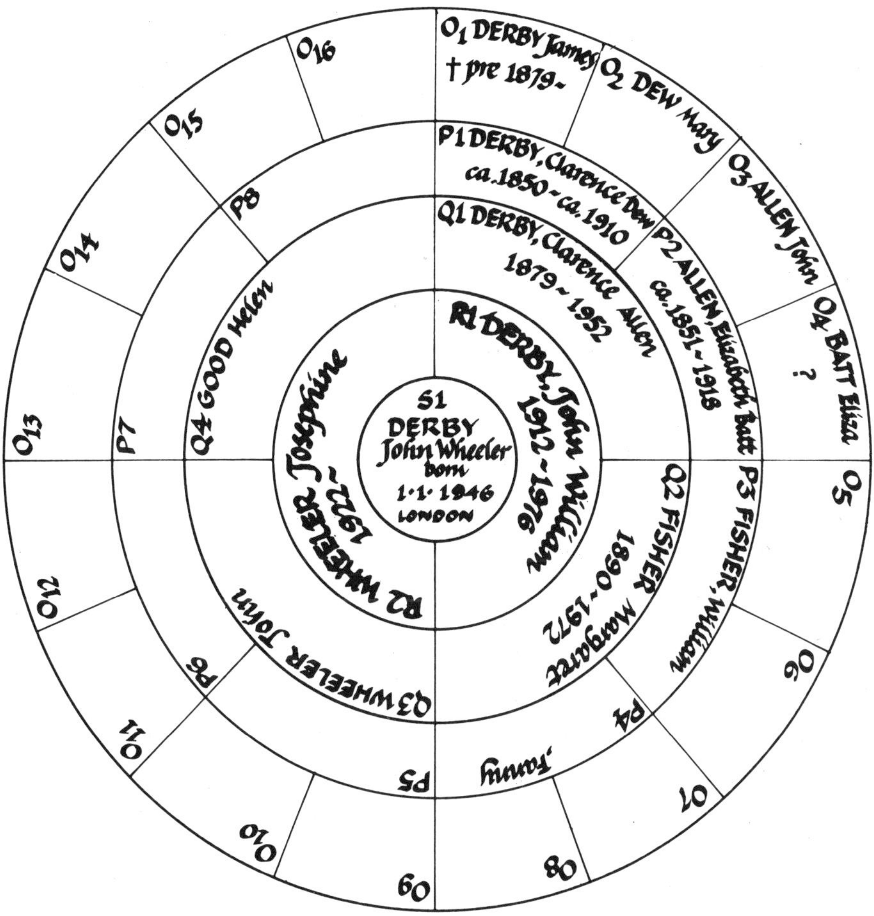

THE GENERATION GRID

In the method which is being increasingly adopted, for the referencing of ancestors, each generation is given a grid letter. You may have been advised to call yourself 'S' for 'self', and if you were born between 1920 and 1949, this is correct. (Should it be that you were born in the previous 30 years, i.e. 1890-1919, you should call yourself 'R'). Your parents' generation takes 'R', your grandparents take 'Q', and your great-grandparents take 'P'. It is assumed that the span between 2 generations is 30 years; so you will have reached generation A in the 14th century. Should you discover an ancestor who 'came over' in 1066, you would be at the minus P generation. Your child would be 'T', grandchildren 'U' etc.

As the number of your ancestors doubles in each generation, if you found all of them who lived at the time of William the Conqueror, you would have identified nearly 537 million ancestors. Considering that historians assure us that the 1379 poll-tax return (yes, they too had taxes!) indicated that England only had a population of about 1,355,000 adults, this does not seem to work out. The explanation is that your ancestors intermarried.

In our tree, there were several marriages between different members of the linked branches, but, most inconveniently for drawing up the extended family tree, some did not marry within their own generation grid. This caused some difficulties. Added to this were problems like the one arising from one relative who travelled abroad, and who wanted to ascertain his relationship to that charming lady he met at the party of a second cousin once removed; the only clue he had was her name.

So there was no choice; the grid letter alone was insufficient. A number had to be added to the letter. Taking the circular design of Fig. 5, and then starting at 12 o'clock with number 1, and progressing in a clockwise direction, I allotted a number to each ancestor. The family tree Fig. 3 (page 16) now looked like Fig. 6.

figure 6

The Extended Tree of Figure 4 Using the Generation Grid.

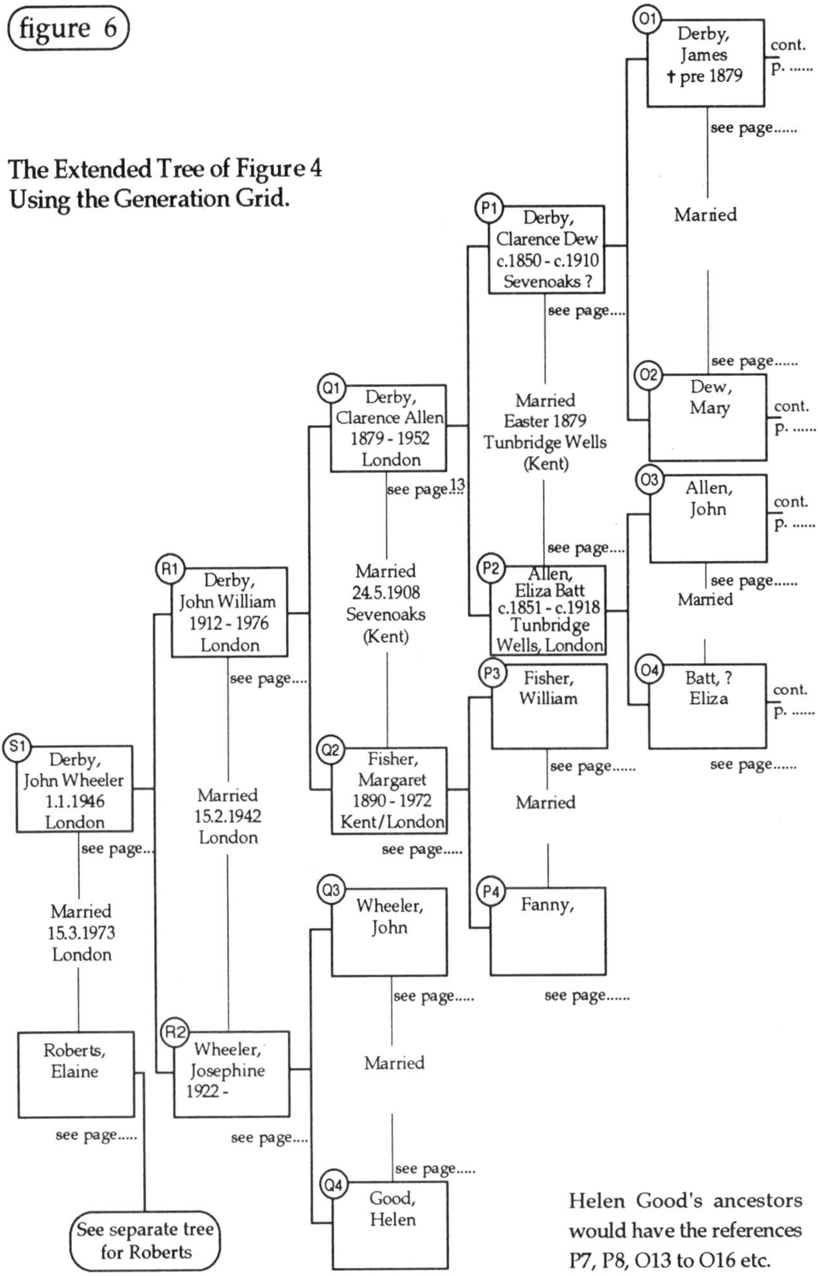

Helen Good's ancestors would have the references P7, P8, O13 to O16 etc.

When it came to the loose leaf sheets of the ancestors, with the trees of their offspring, they would take their own generation grid letter followed by an O for offspring, the reference of the father and then their position in their immediate family.

figure 7

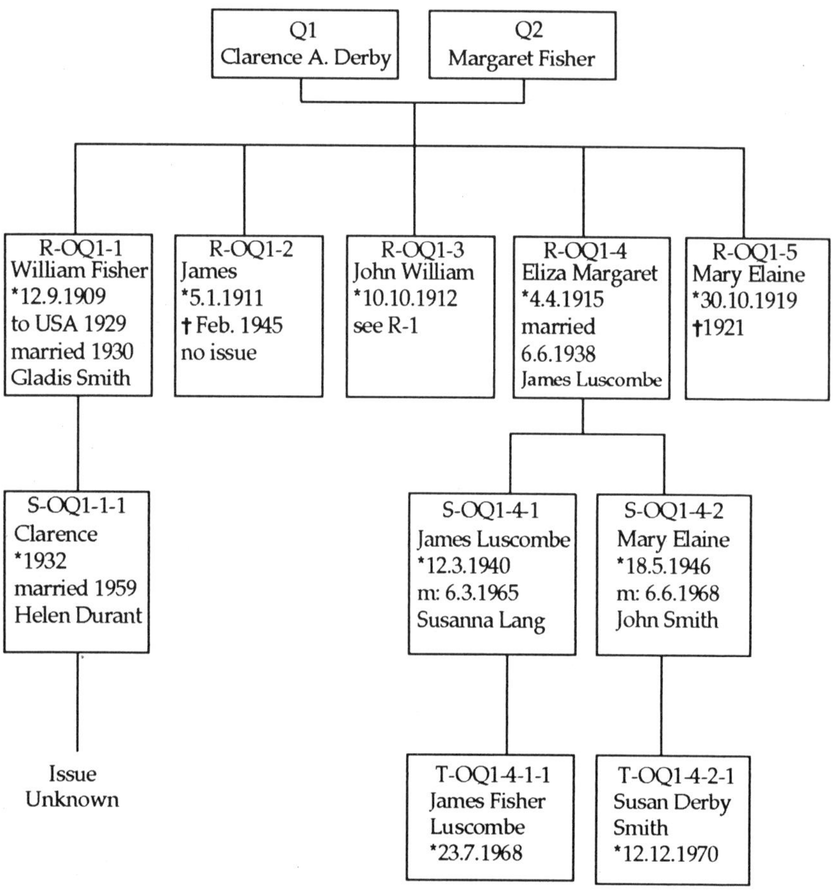

NB Note that R-OQ1-3 becomes R1 because he is the direct ancestor of John Wheeler Derby (S1)

The droptree (Fig. 7) is drawn on the loose leaf sheet of Clarence A. Derby (see Fig. 2, page 13), and space is left at the bottom for future additions.

To avoid the complication and danger of getting muddled in the numbering of pages, I give only one number to each person, when the first loose-leaf page is used. I add a.b.c.d.,etc. to further pages relating to the same person and to those of his offspring who are not direct ancestors.

Under this scheme, 'S-OQ1-1-2' is your first cousin, the second child of his parents, one of whom is the elder sibling of one of your parents. The further the letter following O is from your own, the more distant is your relationship to the person in question. In the case of mixed generations, I give the female partner 2 references, her own and that of her husband, adding an Sp for spouse. Her children follow her husband's reference.

I adopted this method because I have found that, in our widely spread family, the Generation Grid is more convenient. Children and grandchildren could be easily accommodated, without having to draw up new trees all the time.

ANCESTORS WHO REMARRIED

It is frequently found that ancestors, having lost their spouses - mostly through death - remarry, and that can lead to very complicated situations, Particularly when later, part-related or unrelated offspring of this new couple intermarry. As stated before, the researching descendant ignores all the complexities, following the line of biological parents, but still records all ancestors involved. The tree resulting from such a situation could look like this:

figure 8

Judith -------- (1) -------- Jeremy -------- (2) -------- Isabella -------- (1) -------- Peter

1715 Elizabeth	1725 Mary	1719 Jonathan

Here, Jeremy first married Judith, and they had a daughter Elizabeth. Judith died. Isabella was first married to Peter, and they had a son Jonathan. Peter died also. The widowed Isabella and Jeremy married, producing daughter Mary.

Mary is a half-sister to both Elizabeth and Jonathan, but Jonathan and Elizabeth are biologically unrelated, although others may think them to be siblings, because they grew up in the same household, having the same family name. Jonathan established his right to the name simply by using it, as an alias, a practice which is quite legal, even without formal adoption, as long as authorities such as the Taxation Department are aware of the situation, so that there is no cover-up.

For the index, I use a spreadsheet, simply because I thereby can put it all into alphabetical order without too much trouble but a card-index would do just as well. Consideration of this matter raises the next significant question:

IS A COMPUTER NEEDED?

The answer is a categorical 'No', although having one will come in handy. If you do not have access to a computer but would like to buy one, just for this hobby, then firstly find out what equipment others have, what they do with it, and how they like it. Find out what programmes (software) are on the market, before you decide on what hardware (computer, drive, etc.) to buy. There are good specialist books, on the topic, for family historians to read. You may find out all that you need to know about it in your local FHS, if it is a larger one, as most have a computer interest group. There is one at the SoG in London, which produces its own journal. The Family Tree Magazine (FTM hereafter) now incorporates some pages on computers in every issue. I was given, as a gift, a software package for genealogy, developed for my computer. I played around with it and decided to stay with what I had already developed myself, as it suited my needs better.

David Hawgood, who edits the Computer Section of the FTM, has written several books on computers in genealogy. The most useful one for the beginner might well be 'Computers for Family

History'. David can be contacted at 26 Cloister Road, Acton, London W3 ODE, England.

An excellent article published in the FTM Oct. 1994 Vol 10 No 12 p. 38 includes a table of genealogy programs for the computer listing their capabilities.

BIRTHS-DEATHS-MARRIAGES

In the lives of people, these are the three major events which are registered and which are used in compiling the skeleton of the family tree. In the USA they are called 'vital statistics'.

They are largely in the hands of the State. Even in England, where marriages can be legally performed by going only to the Church, the entries are still recorded in the state's registers.

AUSTRALIA

In Australia, a relatively young country, it is quite easy to find the records, in the Capital City of each state. If the details are known and the documents are not covered by laws of privacy, the certificates can simply be ordered from the Registrar's office.

Civil registration started at different times in different states, but generally only a few years after each colony was established. For instance, in South Australia, which received no convicts, 1836 was the year of the Colony's foundation and the State Registers started on the first of July 1842. In the few intervening years, registers were kept only by the churches.

Increasing numbers of indexes of old church registers and of civil registrations are being published and there are others in existence. Depending on the State laws, they may be consulted by the public, if the event occurred in the 19th Century, and they can be found in the State Archives and/or State Reference Libraries as well as in larger FHS libraries.

The indexes of the registers give varying information, depending on state and period, but this information, of itself, is generally insufficient to establish whether one has actually found the person being researched, unless one already knows the exact date and place of the event, or the name is very rare. The only way to find out, for certain, is to buy the certificate.

One can find indexes covering the Registers of the Australian States over the following periods, where * refers to birth, bap to baptism, m to marriage, d to death and b to burial:

NSW * 1856–1905; bap 1788–1855; m 1788–1905;
d 1856–1905; b 1788–1855.

NT * and m and d: 1870–1902.

QLD * 1850–1904; bap 1829–1856; m 1856–1914; d 1856–1914.

SA * 1842–1906; m 1842–1916; d 1842–1915.

TAS * 1838–1899; bap 1803–1933; m 1803–1899; d 1838–1899;
b 1803–1933.

VIC * 1853–1913; bap 1834–1853; m 1837–1930; d 1853–1960;
b 1837–1853.

WA * 1841–1905; bap 1829–1841; m 1829–1906; d 1841–1905.

In South Australia, the Births, Deaths & Marriages Registration Office, Chesser House, 91 Grenfell Street, Adelaide SA 5000 (GPO Box 1351 Adelaide SA 5001) provides certificates. However, due to the law concerning the right to privacy, there are limitations and the indexes are no longer open to the public. Those which refer to events prior to the early 1900s can be found in the Mortlock Library, North Terrace, Adelaide 5000, as well as at the South Australian Genealogy and Heraldry Society (SAGHS hereafter), 201 Unley Road, Unley SA 5061 (GPO Box 592, Adelaide SA 5001). The latter also has some printed indexes related to personal notices from old newspapers, increasing amounts of data extracted from such notices in *The Advertiser*, and much more besides.

After searches of all relevant libraries in Adelaide, a visit to the State Archives, 55 King William Road, North Adelaide 5006 (phone 267 8220) may be useful.

There are also Commonwealth Archives at 11 Derlanger Avenue, Collinswood SA 5081 (phone 08 269 0100). It is wise to phone before a visit, to ascertain opening hours.

The Northern Territory was administered originally by South Australia, so a search related to that region should begin with the SAGHS and the Mortlock Library, North Terrace, Adelaide, before Darwin itself, unless the latter town is within easier reach. The pre - 1863 records for the Territory are held by NSW. There are two sources of information in Darwin itself: The Registrar-General, Registry of Births, Deaths and Marriages, PO Box 3021, Darwin NT 0801. Northern Territory Archives Service, corner of Carey Street and McMinn Street, Darwin NT 0800.

In New South Wales the Registrar, Registry of Births, Deaths and Marriages, can be reached at GPO Box 30, Sydney NSW 2001. The State Archives are at 2 Globe Street, The Rocks, Sydney NSW 2000. There is also The Library of Australian History, 17 Mitchell Street, North Sydney NSW 2059.

In Queensland, for records from 1890 onwards, contact the Registrar-General, Births, Deaths and Marriages, PO Box 188, Albert Street, Brisbane QLD 4002. For records prior to 1890, write to the State Archivist, PO Box 1397, Sunnybank Hills QLD 4109. The Queensland State Archives are at 435 Compton Road, Runcorn QLD 4113.

In Tasmania, the actual certificates until 1899 can be viewed after registration numbers have been found on microfiche. For records after 1899, one should contact the Registrar-General, Registry of Births, Deaths and Marriages, PO Box 198, Hobart TAS 7001.

In Victoria, the address of the Registry of Births, Deaths and Marriages is PO Box 4332, Melbourne VIC 3001. The Public Records Office of Victoria is at 57 Cherry Lane, Laverton, North Victoria 3028.

In Western Australia, The Registrar-General's Office can be contacted at PO Box 7720, Cloisters Square WA 6850. The State Archives, library and information service of WA, are in the Perth Cultural Centre, WA 6000.

For the Australian Capital Territory, write to the Registrar of Births, Deaths and Marriages at PO Box 788, Canberra ACT 2601, for records after 1930 only.

The National Library is at the Queanbeyan City Council, Canberra.

There is now, in some places, a movement towards 'decentralisation', not only in Australia, but also in England. In South Australia, the District Records of Births 1842 - 1906, Marriages 1842 - 1916 and Deaths 1842 - 1967 have been committed to the care and custody of libraries within the former registration districts. These records are accessible to the public under certain conditions. All the information about this, with addresses and opening hours, is laid out in an article by Maureen M Leadbeater, in the South Australian Genealogist, Vol. 21, No. 1 (January 1994), on pages 8 to 13.

As the information varies not only between States, but also between periods, a birth certificate may give, beside the name and sex of the child and the date and place of birth, it's father's name and occupation and mother's name and maiden name. Some may give even more information.

For a marriage, the certificate will give the names of the spouses and their occupations, and most give the fathers' names. The Australian Institute of Genealogical Studies has published a booklet *Birth, Death and Marriage Certificates in Australia* by Fay Young and Don Harris. It gives the exact information. Copies of indexes may be found in other libraries, such as those of a FHS.

An exhaustive guide *Sources for South Australian History* by Andrew Guy Peake, would be invaluable. Another guide to sources is *Tracing your Family History in Australia* by Nick Vine Hall, who also brought out a second edition *Parish Registers in Australia.* All three books should be on the shelves of every Australian FHS (probably 'NOT for Loan' stamped all over them). This allows one to check or decide which meets one's needs best.

If the informant is knowledgeable, one can use the death certificate as a 'link document'. It will probably give the name, the address, the age, the marital status, the cause of death, the length of the illness, and the name of the doctor and the date when he was last consulted. It may also reveal the names of parents, the places of their birth and the deceased's length of residency in Australia. It may go on to state the age of the person at marriage, the place of the marriage, the name of the spouse, and finally the names and ages of surviving children, as well as the numbers of deceased children of each sex. The name and address of the informant is also given and sometimes the relationship to the deceased. However not all are so exhaustive and they are not necessarily accurate. I saw the death certificates of a husband and wife, who had died 20 years apart. The widow made the declaration for her husband, the grandson for his grandmother. One would expect that 'mother knows best', but the great-grandson of the couple is still trying to find out if he had a great-uncle or a great-aunt, who would have been alive at the time, and the only thing that is matching on both declarations is the middle name of the person in question, which was great-grandmother's maiden name... Yet the young man was reasonably knowledgeable, as the information on both death certificates enabled the researcher to find not only the marriage certificate in England, but also the birth certificates of both parties.

There is a project under way, called AGCI, which stands for Australian Genealogical Computer Index. Its purpose is to index genealogical records throughout Australasia, including New Zealand. This is a long-term project. The resulting microfiche are available at participating Genealogical Societies in Australia and New Zealand. The data entered can be of any nature, as long as they are held by a repository to which the public has some access. The second edition became available late in 1992 and a third was envisaged for 1994. Listed are surname, given name, place, date, event, source and reference. Like the International Genealogical Index (IGI hereafter), this project will become increasingly important as a research tool, as years go by.

ENGLAND

Most people who are interested in family history, and whose ancestors were born into an English speaking tradition no less than 150 years ago, will, sooner or later, search for information in England. In order to help in the finding of the relevant registers from different periods, the following short historical account may be useful.

It was during the reign of Queen Elizabeth I, in the mid 16th-Century, that parish registers began to be kept properly. A mandate to achieve this was issued in 1538, but, as with all new things, it took time. The Queen approved an order in 1597, that registers were to be kept only on parchment. Depending on the size of the parish, the standing of the parson, and the funds available, the registers were kept by the parish priest himself, or the parish clerk, or the verger or maybe even other officials. Entries were not always made on the spot, and sometimes they were even lost on slips of paper hastily pocketed. The parson might disapprove of a parishioner, particularly when she produced the third child for baptism without wanting to cite the father, and then he might vent his feelings in a written comment in the register. On the other hand, a burial entry could also bear a comment on the loss which the community had suffered. So the information given can vary greatly. The records were kept in the church, in the 'Parish Chest', together with all sorts of papers which are very interesting to the family historian and which are mentioned elsewhere. Until relatively recently, these registers could be consulted only by, or with the approval of, the incumbent, the parish priest, who was entitled to a fee. It was gradually realised that these records were not securely housed, and were exposed to vermin, dampness and the like, and gradually all the full registers were deposited in the regional Record Offices or in Public Libraries, where the conditions are much more favourable for their preservation. I remember when we were, in the mid - 1970s, being given the keys to a small and very old country church, to visit. Amongst the memorials to the Lords of the nearby Manor, between two tombs, stood the beautifully carved Parish Chest. We lifted the lid to find the proverbial poor church mouse, dead, on top and next to the most recent register. We sounded the alarm bells and were relieved to find on our next visit that the chest was empty, the parish registers having been transferred to the County Record Office.

Once a year, the incumbent was obliged to copy out all the entries of the ceremonies he had performed during the past year and send the copy to his bishop. These are know as Bishop's Transcripts (BTs hereafter). It is advisable to consult both the parish register and the Bishop's Transcripts. They are identical only in theory. These BTs ceased to be submitted in the late 1800s. Marriages were preceded by banns, and these were also registered, sometimes in a separate book. The variety of registers found in parishes is great. If two people from different parishes were married, banns were published in both parish churches, but the marriage entry was made generally only in the parish in which the ceremony took place. It is a well - known fact that many future spouses moved to the parish, in which the marriage was going to take place just before the ceremony - one month residence was the official requirement - and the entry then stated 'both of this parish'. I have tried for over seventeen years to find an elusive gentleman, who was certainly not born in the parish, unless, of course, someone wrote the details of his baptism on a piece of paper and mislaid it. All the parishes within a twenty-mile radius, in ever increasing circles, were searched, this being the recommended strategy for such cases. I concluded that he belonged to the few who are said, according to a study, to have moved afar, in days when we thought they stayed firmly in their villages, generation after generation.

A way to avoid banns, used since 1533, not only by the well-to-do but also by those, such as widows and nonconformists, who did not like the publicity of them, was by paying a fee to obtain a marriage licence. It was generally the Bishop, and those clerics he appointed for the task, who dispensed the licences, mostly to be used in a designated church on a specific date. Allegations (affidavits) were sworn and bonds (between hundreds and thousands of pounds) were given, in case the marriage proved later to be unlawful. (This was compulsory from 1580.) The documents relevant to these are now mostly in the County Record Offices and should definitely be searched, as they generally give additional information.

The term 'of age' in a parish marriage register generally means twenty-one years old. However, this may also mean that the spouses had reached an age at which parental consent was no longer required and they might be very much older. Cases can be cited, when the spouses were younger, but the parson did not know.

Between 1754 and 1837, marriages, to be legal, had to take place in a Church of England parish church. The only exceptions were for members of the Society of Friends (Quakers) and for Jews, both of whom hold their own records.

During the time of the Commonwealth (in the middle of the 17th century, under Cromwell), the marriage service was replaced by a marriage contract in front of a justice of the peace. This is a difficult period to research.

A major change occurred in March 1837, when the Government took control of the records. All births, deaths and marriages had to be registered and only when marriages were performed in a church could the incumbent priest or minister take the role of the registrar on behalf of the State, afterwards passing on the registers to the proper authorities. For some time, all these documents for England and Wales were held in Somerset House, London, but, due to shortage of space, they transferred much of their material, including the Births, Deaths and Marriages (BDMs hereafter) to St Catherine's House, a few steps away, across The Strand, in Aldwych. Somerset House now holds wills made since 1857, and to search the indexes there is a pleasure. Copies of these indexes are now also available elsewhere.

In St Catherine's House, researching is not as easy. One needs to be prepared to heave the heavy tomes of indexes from the shelves onto search tables, of which there are never enough for the throng of searchers. There are four tomes for each year, each covering the events that were registered – as opposed to occurred – during the previous quarter, without giving the actual dates. The information is scant. For instance, in the death indexes, the family name is put into alphabetical order, as it appears on the register. Then follows the Christian name, the area of death and a reference; one is not even given the exact date of the event, let alone, the age of the deceased for the period before 1866. As from June 1968, the age entry, which is often inaccurate, has been replaced by the date of birth. From the September quarter of 1911, birth indexes show the maiden surname of the mother. Marriages are indexed under both the bride and the groom's names. If both are known to the searcher, both can be checked in the same register by matching references. However, in the case of widows, the name may be mistaken by the searcher. As from the March quarter 1912, the surname of the spouse is also shown. Until August 1946, the reference itself can be of assistance, as it consists of two parts: a code and a number. The code refers to the area in which the event was registered and is given in appendix two. The number refers to its entry. It is, however, important to remember that this reference applies only to St Catherine's registers, not to the corresponding ones in other record offices. These indexes are increasingly available elsewhere, on microform, often for limited years only, mostly in FHS libraries. SAGHS in Adelaide holds the BDM on microfilms 1837–1875 and on microfiche 1876–1910, adding regularly indexes for further years.

Maps of the registration districts have been published by the Institute of Heraldic and Genealogical Studies, in Canterbury Kent. They give more precise information about the Civil Registration Districts, and can be bought through the FTM. A copy (1987 edn) for the period 1837–1851 is in the State Library of Victoria in Melbourne.

There are also some individual Registration Districts for which 1836 maps have been privately produced; e.g. Norfolk, Suffolk and Essex.

Once the references have been found, you can order the certificate on special forms, paying a substantial fee, part of which will be refunded if the staff decides it is not the person you are researching. If they consider it matches your information, you receive a certificate, but it may still not be your relative. Unwanted certificates can be sent to a volunteer who tries to prevent them going to waste. There is a postal service, which is more expensive and slower than when certificates are ordered personally at St Catherine's House, where they can be picked up a day or two later, or sent by mail. The address to which to write for certificates is Postal Application Section, General Register Office, Smedly Hydro, Southport, Merseyside, PR8 2HH.

If you know the exact place of the event, the corresponding

County Register Office (CRO hereafter) may be able to supply certificates more cheaply.

Birth Certificates for England and Wales give the name and sex of the child, the date and place of birth, the names of both parents and the father's occupation, as well as the signature, description and residence of the informant, the date of registration, and the name of the registrar.

The marriage certificate gives the date and place of the ceremony, the celebrant and the witnesses, as well as the names of the spouses, their ages, their 'condition' (eg. if bachelor), rank or profession, their residence at the time of marriage and the names and occupations of the fathers.

Death certificates give date and place, the name of the deceased, the sex, age and occupation, the cause of death, the signature, description and residence of the informant, the date when the death was registered, and the signature of the registrar. Consular Returns (as from 1849) do not give a cause of death. Eve McLaughlin has written three guides: *St Catherine's House; Somerset House Wills* and *Wills before 1858.*

ISLE OF MAN

Civil registration records are available for births and deaths from 1878, and for marriages from 1884. They are kept by the Chief Registrar, General Registry, Finch Road, Douglas, Isle of Man.

LUNDY ISLAND (BRISTOL CHANNEL)

Some birth records for the period between 1831 and 1958 can be found in the Miscellaneous Foreign Returns RG 32 at PRO (indexed RG 43) The same is true for the following Channel Islands:

1. JERSEY

Civil registration has applied since August 1842. Write to the Superintendent Registrar, Judicial Greffe, States' Offices, 10 Hill Street, Royal Square, St Helier, Jersey, Channel Islands.

2. GUERNSEY, JETHOU & HERM

Registration has been in place since 1840. Contact HM Greffier, General Register Office, The Greffe, Royal Court House, St Peter Port, Guernsey, Channel Islands.

3. ALDERNEY

Records for events since1925 are kept at Guernsey. For others, write to the Clerk of the Court, Queen Elizabeth Street, Alderney, Channel Islands.

4. SARK

Records for events since 1925 are kept at Guernsey. For others, write to the Registrar, La Valette, Sark, Channel Islands.

N.B. Anyone searching in any of these islands would do well to study carefully Tom Wood's article in the FTM, October 1993, pages 4 & 5 and FTM August 1994, p15.

SCOTLAND

Civil registration in Scotland started on 1st January 1855 and gave, in that year only, much information. It was partially re-introduced in 1861, providing somewhat more information than St Catherine's House. The records can now be found with the Registrar–General, General Register Office for Scotland, New Register House, Edinburgh, Scotland EH1 3YT. Unlike St Catherine's House and Somerset House in London, they charge a fee here for searching the indexes. On the other hand, a document found may be viewed for a limited time under staff supervision before purchase. If you know at which local register office the event would have been recorded originally, it may be cheaper to search there. Photocopies of a birth, marriage and death certificate have been published in the FTM Vol. 3, No.12, p. 12 (October 1987). It is vital to make reservations well before a visit, as places are limited. For a fee, searches by mail can be made by the staff. There is a comprehensive list of services which will be sent on request with a stamped, addressed envelope (SAE hereafter) or two international reply coupons (IRC hereafter), and the services need to be prepaid.

In 1855, the Registrar called in all previous (old) parish registers of the Church of Scotland, which is Presbyterian. This is of great advantage to the searcher, who is thus saved much travelling. However, some records, mostly church session minutes, appear to have been returned gradually to the safe keeping of local archives.

What one cannot find in the above General Register Office (GRO hereafter) for Scotland, might be in the Register House next door, or vice versa. Fees and conditions vary between these two institutions.

The GRO for Scotland holds many other records, such as all six census returns (1841-1891) and much more. There are several books on the market useful for this area. One of them is *In Search of Scottish Ancestry* by G. Hamilton-Edwards. A list of others, compiled by Donald Whyte. F.H.G., F.S.G., can be found in the FTM Vol. 4, No. 8, p. 7 (June 1988), and in an article by Tom Wood, in the issue of July 1994, p. 14.

Although the General Provincial Council passed an act in 1553, instructing parishes to keep registers, only twenty-two Scottish registers, started before 1600, survive; most do not begin before the 1750s, and some even later. Ten regional parish maps for Scotland can be bought through the FTM.

The beginner is likely to get confused between two Institutions in Edinburgh which are to be found next to each other; there is no danger of going to the wrong place, only the wrong building. First, there was 'The Register House', which became too small; so 'The New Register House' was built. It took over the documents and functions of the BDM Registration amongst other things, but left the archives in the earlier building, which retained its name. This led to confusion among new researchers from afar, who looked for the Old Register House, whose name did not exist. The introduction of the additional title of 'General Register Office for Scotland', with the address 'New Register House' Edinburgh, Scotland, EH1 3YT assists the newcomer. *Here fees are charged.*

The title, 'Scottish Record Office, HM General Register House', Edinburgh, Scotland, EH1 3YY, applies to the archives. *The access to their Search Rooms is free.* There is some overlapping of material, that can be found in both institutions, in which different rules apply.

Books that would help in this field are *Tracing your Scottish Ancestors in the Scottish Record Office* (HMSO) and *Sources for Scottish Genealogy and Family History* by D. J. Steel (SoG).

An account of the new development of computerised indexes, and sufficient instructions about what to do when using them, as well as other helpful advice, can be found in an article by Tom Wood in the July 1993 issue of the FTM, page 42.

Microfilmed copies of 1855–1920 Scottish BDM indexes can be found at the SoG, London.

It is also good to remember that Scottish Law is based on Roman Law, in contrast to England (Common Law) and this affects Landownership. see page 97.

IRELAND

Research in this country has problems all of its own.

Here, more so than elsewhere, it is essential to know the place and date of an event as accurately as possible.

Civil registration began on 1st of January 1864, and records are kept in the General Register Office, 8–11 Lombard Street East, Dublin, EIRE. Here are all birth, death and marriage entries for Ireland 1864–1921 and non-Catholic marriages for Ireland (EIRE) from 1845. There is an index covering thousands of marriage entries between 1845 and 1863 for all Protestant denominations. There are also records for births, marriages and deaths in the Republic of Ireland (EIRE) from 1922.

The National Archives, Four Courts Building, Dublin 7, will send against 3 IRCs, free leaflets on Family History in Ireland. Not all Roman Catholic Registers have survived, particularly in remote country areas. The well-known fire that raged through the buildings in 1922 did not destroy all the documents, as many tend to believe.

It may be useful to remember that in 1869 the Church of Ireland was disestablished, its registers becoming public records.

The Genealogical Office in Kildare Street, Dublin, which advertises only a postal service, has been found to be very helpful to visitors.

All births, deaths and marriages, that occurred in Northern Ireland (ULSTER) from 1922, are held in the office of the Registrar - General for Northern Ireland, General Register Office, Department of Health and Social Services, Oxford House, 49–55 Chichester Street, Belfast, Northern Ireland BT1 4HL.

As in England, if you know precisely the local registry office at which the event was originally registered, more information may be obtained, particularly during a personal visit. Their addresses can be found in regional telephone directories under the heading, 'Health Board'.

Names beginning with O' and Mac should also be searched without these prefixes.

There is some information, for searchers in Ireland, to be found in the British Museum's Library, London. However, before going there, consult the article in the FTM January 1989 issue, on p. 15, to avoid disappointment.

Articles by Tom Wood in the FTM issues of August 1993 (p. 13) September 1993 (p. 8 & 9), and August 1994 (p. 14 & 15) are full of helpful information, as are those by Paul Gorry in the April (p. 21) and November issues (p. 43), 1993.

Donald Begley wrote three books on search in Ireland. They are *The Ancestor Trail in Ireland, Handbook on Irish Genealogy* and *Irish Genealogy, A Record Finder*.

NEW ZEALAND

The registration of European births, deaths and marriages began in 1848, and in 1856 registration was made compulsory. The

National Registers are held at the Registrar General's Office (RGO), Levin House, 191 High Street, Lower Hutt, N.Z., telephone Wellington 569 4487 (under Justice Department).

The National Archives of New Zealand are at 10 Mulgrave Street, PO Box 12050, Thorndon, Wellington 6083, and have Regional Offices throughout the country. Their services are outlined on page 348 of the *NZ Genealogist* Sept/Oct 1992, with an update in the March/April 1993 issue, pages 92 to 94.

A very helpful book to research in this country is *Tracing Family History in New Zealand*. It was written in 1988 by Anne Bromell, and published by G.P. Books, Wellington, New Zealand.

USA

Public Records.

As for elsewhere, public officials do not search records for the genealogists; even less do they evaluate the usefulness to the person who enquires. However, if they hold specifically named records (name, date, place, type of event), they will give a certified copy of the relevant document, if the appropriate fee has been paid.

Most states began keeping 'vital statistics', as well as wills, probate records, deeds, marriage licences and bonds as from 1900. Some started in 1850. New England has records dating from 1630, and many of those very early ones have been printed. Originally, records were deposited in the county house court. Others were kept at town level, and some filed duplicate copies later with the State Board of Health or similar authorities.

Certified copies can be obtained from the county clerk or from the State Department of Health, at prices which make people buying them in Australia and England green with envy. The Superintendent of Documents, Government Printing Office, Washington D.C. 20402, will provide material giving details of the US Public Health Service. It lists the exact addresses of the various offices supplying such certificates, and also outlines the fees charged by them.

The following four publications can be requested:

- Where to write for birth and death records.
- Where to write for marriage records.
- Where to write for divorce records.
- Where to write for birth and death records of US citizens who were born and died outside of the USA and for birth certificates for alien children adopted by US citizens.

CHURCH RECORD KEEPERS

Locating church records in the USA is very complicated, due to the great variety of denominations and sects. The difficulty is compounded by the absence of a state church, like the Church of England.

Many ministers serve large circuits, travelling far, and recording the details of ceremonies in their home parish registers, or in their own personal records.

These records are mostly found in the local churches, unless they have been transferred to central church archives or church historical societies. When you are looking for the original church records, if the congregation is still active, it is best to contact the pastor or lay official of the congregation. They either have the records or know where they are. Public record offices, libraries and local history societies may hold those of defunct congregations. Some of the private records of ministers may have been inherited by their descendants, or they may be in other private hands or with public or municipal authorities.

Early records, particularly those of New England congregations, have been commonly printed in volume form. Early originals may be hard to read, but where translations were involved, they may not have the errors that could have occurred during transcription.

A recent publication for research in the USA, that includes maps of migration trails, is the *Handybook for Genealogists* (8th edition Everton Publishers Inc., P.O. Box 368, LOGAN UT 8432-0368 USA.

VISITING LIBRARIES AND RECORD OFFICES

Every institution has its own rules but many have common features.

The old rule of absolute silence in libraries may no longer be adhered to as rigidly as in the past, as librarians increasingly talk at normal volume. However, it is essential to remember that people are there to do research, so some level of quietness must prevail.

No visit can be really rewarding, unless it is well prepared.

LOCAL PUBLIC LIBRARIES

All have varying opening hours, generally requiring a Reader's Ticket only when books are to be borrowed. Most have an area for 'Reference Books', where one can sit and work with books that are often not for loan. Increasing numbers of libraries have one or more computers to aid the visitor to find material available, and instructions are printed nearby for the user. If your own computer has a 'return' key and the library one has not, then use the 'entry' key instead. Don't be frightened if you have never used such a machine; treat it like a typewriter, with which you are talking, via a screen, which takes the place of a patient librarian. When in trouble, ask a live one.

Increasing numbers of libraries have 'local history' sections, some going so far as having separate buildings for them.

If you live nearby, it is useful to visit the library to see the layout and to ascertain what is there which is of interest to your research.

Inter-library loan is very helpful in many instances, in order to provide books only available from other public libraries.

In the USA, there are also 'Bibliographical Centres' through which smaller centres can contact larger ones to locate certain materials. They are regional, and can be located in the telephone directories. One of the large ones is Pacific North-West Bibliographic Centre, University of Washington Library, Seattle, Washington 98105.

LARGER PUBLIC LIBRARIES AND RECORD OFFICES

If you live afar, you should always ring or write to the library before making a visit, and ask for information concerning opening hours. Make an appointment if you are likely to need special books or fiche and a reader. These are now available in an increasing number of libraries, particularly in England. You will have access to none, unless you have a desk or machine booked. You therefore must state in your request, for an appointment, what you are actually searching for, ask the cost - if any - involved, and ascertain whether you need a reader's ticket. Don't forget to add a large SAE for the answer. You may, in response to your request, receive a reader's ticket or an application form, stating costs. Some libraries require a photograph; the British Library Manuscript Collection needs two recent colour photographs, passport size, to endorse a reader's ticket. On the other hand, English libraries work together and only one card is needed for all belonging to a particular group. You are likely to receive some printed information leaflets concerning your research area. Some libraries produce booklets which they offer for sale at cost price. If you intend to stay for more than a short visit, they are good value and should be carefully studied beforehand, in order to save time.

This approach is necessary for all institutions to which you need access. Do not expect to arrive from many thousand miles away and find an empty desk or reader awaiting you, or presume that waving your international passport will produce a reader's ticket. They will also require a formal document giving your home address.

For instance, I arrived for the first time at the Public Record Office (PRO hereafter) Chancery Lane, in London, WC 2A 1LR, unaware of this, fortunately just after opening time. The gatekeeper directed me to the Office next to him, where I was treated most courteously. I produced my passport, safe in the feeling that this would be most adequate. Not for long! Fortunately, I had my international driver's licence containing my photograph and home address, and both passport and licence were duly recorded. Had I a reference? I must have looked blank. 'Why are you coming here?, I was asked. I produced my prepared sheet about what I wanted to search. This was scanned and the information put down on my application, which I signed (I found later I should have completed that myself beforehand). Then I was given some literature, to study later, a map which showed me where to go and a reader's ticket, all at no cost. The reader's ticket has a number and the PRO will declare arbitrarily when certain numbers become obsolete and need to be renewed, generally some years later. The reader's ticket from the PRO Chancery Lane is also valid in the PRO Kew (Ruskin Avenue, Kew, Richmond, Surrey TW9 4DU) that mostly holds Departmental Records.

Pre - 1858 probate, medieval, legal and non-conformist's records are amongst those at Chancery Lane. They both produce many leaflets, giving the topic required and listing books which cost a few pounds but which will help the searcher to find documents more easily. *Tracing your ancestors in the PRO* by Jane Cox & T Padfield (HMSO), should be studied before going to London. Its 4th Edition (by Amanda Bevan and Andrea Duncan) was published by HMSO in 1991.

Jane Cox latest publication, *Never been here before? A first time guide for Family Historians at the PRO.* (HMSO) can be obtained through the FTM postal book service or from PRO publications Chancery Lane. London WC24 1LR.

The fact that PRO Kew has been greatly enlarged and the documents from PRO Chancery Lane and the PRO outstore at Hayes are going to be transferred to PRO Kew (which is said to commence in September 1995) should not affect the usefulness of these publications. It will be essential during this period of transfer to ring the PRO, London 0181-876-34444 Ext 2-882 to learn if and where documents that used to be at Chancery Lane can be consulted. Only the census returns will remain, at least for the present, at Chancery Lane.

Readers now have plastic swipe cards which they use in the new system installed at Kew, and which allow them to order documents through computers as well as gaining access to various parts of the building. This also assists the staff in assessing the frequency with which given documents are consulted, enabling them to improve further the service provided.

The turnstiles will open automatically in case of emergency. The PRO complex at Kew contains a restaurant.

I was told that the British Museum's Library requires at least one reference. Students get these from their University professors; other researchers can request them from the Institution for which they research, a parish priest or someone similar. One must arrive before opening hours and queue in order to secure a place. Applications for a reader's ticket should be made at the Reader Admission Office, The British Library, Great Russell Street, London WC1B 3DG.

St Catherine's and Somerset House do not require readers' tickets. However, if you visit to buy copies of certificates, take cash. They do accept cheques with postal requests without difficulties, but if you order on the spot, a cheque will only be accepted when a corresponding credit card is produced, for verification. This practice is becoming increasingly prevalent in England.

Apart from a reader's ticket and an appointment, you would be well advised to be thoroughly prepared, in order to get the most from a visit. Write into your bound notebook a 'shopping list' of items which you might be able to find in the institution which you are visiting. List them in order of importance and also in the order in which they may be found in similar documents. For instance, when you decide to look at the IGI, group the names to be researched by area, (e.g. county) and then by name. For St Catherine's House, divide your queries according to births, deaths and marriages; then group by quarters of years, in chronological sequence; finally, arrange them by names in alphabetical order. Leave space on your lists for your findings, and if the information is not found note that also. Make sure that you search thoroughly and do not overlook an item. It happens so easily. Many people say that they cannot research beyond an hour or two without losing concentration, whilst others can work from opening time to closing time. Institutions provide increasingly not only toilet facilities, but also refreshment areas, where you can buy a cup of coffee or tea and eat your own, previously prepared sandwiches.

The original parish registers and documents are in chronological and not in alphabetical order. Before looking at these, it is recommended that you make an alphabetical list of all names to be researched, as a check in times of doubt. Most people work faster by starting at page one at the top and finishing at the bottom of the last page, than by working backwards. However, there are advantages in working from the back, as a variation in the spelling of a name new to the searcher may be spotted earlier.

For this reason, whenever practical, it is better to start with the BTs, as they come in yearly bundles, each bundle giving all the births, deaths and marriages for the designated year in the specified parish. The notes will be titled with date and place (e.g. CRO Exeter, if you are searching in Devon), and there will be a label on the box (e.g. BT Stoke Damerel, which could be the parish searched). Here a start with the most recent year is best and one can work backwards, adding the new names of the brides to the check list, and copying, exactly as written, every event that has occurred for every person bearing any family name, or its variation, on the list. The extraction of every entry for a given name from an index is known as a blanket search, and I use this method in case of an unusual name, thus avoiding having to go back to the same records, unless a transcription error is suspected.

At home, it would be a good idea to try to make family trees from that information.

The next step would be to go to the West Devon Record Office (WDRO herafter) in Plymouth, where the Parish records of Stoke Damerel are stored. There start with the baptismal register corresponding to the timespan and extract all the relevant entries, exactly as found. Then go to the marriage, death and burial registers. If not all entries of the marriages are found. the banns book should be searched, and finally the marriage licences, bonds and allegations at the Devon CRO in Exeter. All these need to be copied exactly or photocopies of the filmed documents be bought, when this is possible.

Then it should be possible to draw family trees with more confidence. The dates of the deaths or burials should make it easier to find the wills, which also would be likely to be at the CRO, unless the deceased had property in more than one diocese before 1857. In that case, the wills of the Prerogative Court of Canterbury (PCC hereafter) or Prerogative Court of York (PCY hereafter) will need to be searched. These are being indexed in increasing numbers.

These wills could then provide one of several 'link documents' which would be needed to establish a tree with confidence.

The staffs of Libraries and Record Offices are employed to care for the documents in their charge and to repair, restore and catalogue them. People may have access to the librarians but they are not really employed to research for the public. They will help as much as possible, but due to limited funding, from which the vast majority of libraries suffer, such assistance is limited. Elderly researchers will tell you how things have changed, and not for the better, and this is largely due to the fact that there is a rapidly increasing number of people wanting access and help. Librarians have been heard to complain bitterly about some of the treatment which they have received, and to deplore the fact that so many visitors come ill-prepared; they cannot assist them as efficiently as searchers who know exactly what they want and need only to be directed to the location.

There is a guide to the many different CROs in England and Wales, *Record Offices: How to find them* (FFHS) by Jeremy Gibson.

American Library Directory (R. R. Bowker Co., New York) gives a complete listing of libraries in the USA and Canada.

Directory of Historical Societies and Agencies in the USA and Canada is a biennial publication by the American Association for State and Local History, 1315 Eighth Avenue South, Nashville, Tennesee 37203.

The Canadian Library Association in Ottowa has published a *Canadian Library Directory.*

INTERNATIONAL GENEALOGICAL INDEX

One of the most useful tools in the search for birth and marriage entries is the IGI compiled by the Church of Jesus Christ of Latter Day Saints, which is also known as LDS Church, or Mormons. Because of their religious beliefs, all adherents are expected to research their ancestors, and they have an ever growing library of information in their centre at Salt Lake City, Utah, USA. They photograph on microfilm, with the permission of the church authority holding the various birth and marriage registers, all documents, page by page. The entries are then computerised twice, and the two sets of information are compared. Any discrepancies are checked by a third person, who then amends the faulty entries or evaluates those which are difficult to decipher with certainty. The entries treated thus are marked with a sign given at the bottom of each page; the Greek letter *sigma* means 'evaluated entry' in the old indexes, and the Greek letter *delta* signifies 'entry altered from source' in more recent editions. The resulting printouts are then photographed on to 'microfiche' and one can use a special 'reader' in order to search these fiche for the desired entry. Fortunately, one need not be a Mormon to use these fiche. An increasing number of Record Offices (RO hereafter), libraries and FHSs buy the fiche covering their own areas of research, and every library of the LDS Church, worldwide, has at least the fiche covering its own area and, sometimes, those for the whole of the world. This is a mammoth task which is far from being completed.

The new editions appear approximately every four years. Theoretically, they should contain all entries of previous editions. However, this may not necessarily be so. 'Controlled extraction records' are checked, to see if ordnance work has really been completed. If it has not, the entries under question are removed from the new edition. Such questions arise mainly because of entries from miscellaneous sources, like private ancestral research, rather than from those which originate in the registers. Some institutions may have the new edition on compact disks for use on computers.

The 1988 edition held only 60% of the parishes of Devon in England, and this county is better covered than others. The incompleteness is due not only to the enormous amount of work involved, but also because not all church authorities allow their registers to be microfilmed. In addition, the cost is considerable, even if all the manpower is unpaid. So a charge is levied that varies from place to place. The LDS Church, itself asks for no fee, but the searcher is expected to make an appropriate donation. There is a fixed charge for printouts and material that the church library orders from Salt Lake City on request, such as the film of a parish register, which enables the researcher to see the entire entry. The church library has a special set of fiche detailing the books they hold in Salt Lake City, and those which may be ordered from there. There are accredited researchers who do work there, for a fee, but anyone can travel to Salt Lake City and research in the library. The list of local libraries can be found in the telephone book.

Before researching the IGI, it is recommended that those, who want to get the most out of it, should first read the instructions, now mostly on fiche and supplied by the LDS Church with all copies.

Before using the IGI for Wales, it is essential to read the article, 'Using the IGI for Wales and Monmouth' by Chris Pitt Lewis, published in the Gwent F H Journal of April 1982. This article appears also in the *Gibson Guide* called *General Register Office and the International Genealogical Indexes* (1987). This guide is very useful for English research. The author has produced a series of very helpful publications, which he updates and renames periodically.

The LDS Church provides also a Family Registry Service free of charge, throughout the world. The registration of the surname can be made through the post but only on their printed forms. This is then recorded on microfiche. To extract addresses of others researching a given name, from the fiche, one needs to go to one of the LDS Family History Centres of Genealogical Libraries.

There is no need to fear using the IGI on religious grounds. It is stressed continuously that there is no transfer of information between the genealogical libraries and the 'missionary' department of the LDS Church. You may be invited to share the information you hold about your ancestors, but there is no pressure applied. I, myself, once wrote direct to Salt Lake City, asking if they would please check for additional information on a specific entry, of which I gave full reference from the fiche. I received by way of answer, some printed information concerning their services - including the request for information, if I was prepared to give it - and an explanation why the entry was declared 'uncleared'. I also received guidance about where to look for an answer to my question. In my thank you letter, I explained that I regretted not being able to give them my family information on religious grounds, that I had, however, submitted a copy of my findings to the Society of Genealogists in London and that I would be happy to answer any question of a fellow researcher. I got a very kind answer, telling me more about where I could search further. I immediately sent a thank you note, including the postage for the last letter, which I had promised to do, just in case of such an event.

There are fiche with each edition, giving exact details of which parishes have been covered, and to what extent, and a fiche called *The Parish and Vital Listings*. Not all libraries possess these. *The Phillimore Atlas and Index of Parish Registers*, edited by C. R. Humphery-Smith, is another source for this information in England, but you must first look at the date of publication (not reprint) of this very useful work, because it may not cover the additions of the latest IGI edition. It is a valuable guide.

THE LAYOUT OF THE IGI

The first division of the IGI is geographical, country by country. Then it is subdivided into particular areas. Ireland is divided into counties. Scotland was divided first in the 1984 edition. England is divided into counties. 'London' embraces parts of what was Middlesex, Essex, Kent and Surrey. There were boundary changes in 1974, so you need to be flexible in your search. The IGI uses the old boundaries, as used before 1974.

There are also changes in the names of counties, such as Cumbria and Cumberland; so an atlas is good to have at hand.

Eventually, in any search, specialised and old maps will be needed; these can be found in local or large public reference libraries. In England, there are specialists who sell copies of these; they advertise in FHS Journals and the FTM.

The next division is alphabetical, by family name, where the names that are pronounced identically are grouped together. For instance Liscom, Liscomb, Liscombe, Liscome and Liscoome, as well as all variants of Lyscom and also Liscam, Liscumbe and Liskcombe are all grouped together, but not with Luscomb, etc. At the end of some fiche is a list of names and the page numbers on which they appear. Once you discover how to find this quickly, it can save much time. It may give clues to the whereabouts of an elusive ancestor who may be hiding, as the name may have been badly recorded - the scribe may have misheard, or was deaf, or could not spell properly, or thought he knew better because he was familiar with a similar but different name.

English nobility gives additional problems as the family name differs generally from the title. For instance, the family name of a certain Earl of Salisbury, whose own name was Cecil and whose son's name was John. could be found under Cecil OR Salisbury. Major could be a military rank or a given name, like Duke, Earl, etc.

Next, the given names are put into rigorous alphabetical order. A girl called Beth or Betty could have been baptised Elizabeth, Eliza, Elizabetha, Eliz, etc., every one listed separately, Eliz, the abbreviation, being the first. To complicate matters, Elisabeth is listed separately from Elizabeth. This division is found in the first column under *Name.*

The second column is headed 'Father, Mother, Spouse'.

In the case of a baptism, sometimes only the name of the father is given, but the majority give both parents. If only the mother is given, followed by 'uncleared', it *may* indicate an illegitimate birth. Just the child's name, followed by an empty space, indicates a foundling. It was such an entry, linked with dates and places that did not quite match, that made me think it would be best to investigate this possibility. So I wrote to Salt Lake City, as explained at the beginning of this chapter. I received a photocopy of the relevant page of the parish register to find that a person had entered, in the three columns, about 70 names of baptised children, punctuated by dates, on a single page. It was an obvious and, fortunately, rare occurrence, caused by a negligent registrar, who could have been the verger, parish clerk or even the parson, himself, who, in the end, has to bear the responsibility for such a state of affairs. In this case, the wills solved my problem.

In the case of a marriage, the name of the spouse is given.

This information is followed by 2 columns, each holding one letter only.

The first makes clear the sex of the person:

F female

M male

H husband

W wife

The second gives the type of event:

A adult christening

B birth

C christening, and adults may be included here.

D death or burial, used for infants before they were baptised.

NB: *other deaths are not included*

F birth or christening of the first known child, used instead of a marriage date, when this is unkown.

M marriage

LAVERS, WILLIAM

PAGE 23,981

COUNTRY ENGLAND   COUNTY: DEVON   AS OF MAR 1992

NAME	FATHER / MOTHER OR SPOUSE OR RELATIVE	M=MALE F=FEMALE H=HUSBAND W=WIFE	TYPE	EVENT DATE	TOWN, PARISH	B	C	$	SOURCE BATCH/FILM No	SOURCE SERIAL/SHEET
LAVERS, WILLIAM										
LAVERS, WILLIAM	SPOUSE: WILLMOT MADOCKES/	M	S	24NOV1621	DEAN PRIOR	20OCT1982OG	14FEB1987OG		E050811	0457
LAVERS, WILLIAM	WILLMOT MADOCKES	H	M	24NOV1621	DEAN PRIOR			24FEB1978IF	M050811	0244
LAVERS, WILLIAM	WILLIAM LAVERS/	M	C	21MAR1622	DEAN PRIOR	03OCT1974PV	22NOV1974PV	18DEC1974PV	C050811	0907
LAVERES, WILLIAM	ROBERTE LAVERES/	M	C	11AUG1638	TOTNES	CHILD	CHILD	24MAR1976SG	C051751	5945
LAVERS, WILLIAM	WILLIAM LAVERS/ELIZABETH	M	C	19JAN1639	SLAPTON	26SEP1974LG	11JAN1975LG	12FEB1975LG	C052001	0420
LAVERS, WILLIAM	WILLIAM LAVERS/	M	C	06FEB1641	TOTNES	09DEC1975SG	18MAR1976SG	24MAR1976SG	C051751	6266
LAVERS, WILLIAM	JOHN LAVERS/MARY	M	C	30MAY1641	PLYMPTON ERLE	31MAY1975LA	03JUL1975LA	25JUL1975LA	C051521	0572
LAVERS, WILLIAM	SPOUSE: DORITHIE EBSWORTHIE/	M	S	03FEB1644	PLYMPTON SAINT MARY	23MAR1983LA	06MAY1983LA		E051971	1236
LAVERS, WILLIAM	DORITHIE EBSWORTHIE	H	M	03FEB1644	PLYMPTON SAINT MARY			14MAR1978AZ	M051971	0667
LAVERS, WILLIAM	WILL LAVERS/ELIZABETH	M	C	25DEC1645	SLAPTON	26SEP1974LG	11JAN1975LG	12FEB1975LG	C052001	0548
LAVERS, WILLIAM	SPOUSE: MARY CHAFFE/	M	S	23JUL1655	DEAN PRIOR	20OCT1982OG	14FEB1987OG		E050811	0716
LAVERS, WILLIAM	MARY CHAFFE	H	M	23JUL1655	DEAN PRIOR			24FEB1978IF	M050811	0385
LAVERS, WILLIAM	JOHN LAVERS/MARIE	M	C	23MAR1667	PLYMPTON SAINT MARY	18DEC1975SG	31MAR1976SG	02APR1976SG	C051971	3268
LAVERS, WILLIAM	GILES LAVERS/	M	C	20FEB1671	DEAN PRIOR	04OCT1974PV	22NOV1974PV	18DEC1974PV	C050811	1524
LAVERSE, WILLIAM	WILLIAM LAVERSE/	M	C	08MAY1671	TOTNES	10DEC1975SG	19MAR1976SG	25MAR1976SG	C051751	7850
LAVERS, WILLIAM	CHRISTOFER LAVERS/	M	C	25FEB1676	YEALMPTON	CHILD	CHILD	16JAN1975LA	C052221	1746
LAVERSE, WILLIAM	LUCRETIA ROWE	H	M	02APR1678	BUCKLAND MONACHORUM			05JUL1978SL	M050061	0940
LAVERS, WILLIAM	WILMOTH DYER	H	M	28FEB1682	MARLDON			21DEC1942SL	A184727	0433
LAVERS, WILLIAM @	SPOUSE: WILMOTH DYER/	M	M	28FEB1682	OF MARLDON	28OCT1933LG	PRE-1970	PRE-1970	0177919	FILM
LAVERS, WILLIAM	ROBERT LAVERS/	M	C	03FEB1683	EXETER, SAINT GEORGE	CHILD	CHILD	16JUL1974IF	C050931	0182
LAVERSE, WILLIAM	WILLIAM LAVERSE/LUCRETIA	M	C	06OCT1683	BUCKLAND MONACHORUM	09MAR1974IF	30MAY1974IF	04JUN1974IF	C050061	3507
LAVERS, WILLIAM	PHILLIP LAVERS/ELIZABETH	M	C	07MAR1692	MALBOROUGH	09NOV1974PV	11JAN1975PV	11FEB1975PV	C051341	4987
LAVERS, WILLIAM	EBOTT TORR	H	M	04JUN1694	DEAN PRIOR			24FEB1978IF	M050811	0546
LAVERS, WILLIAM	SARAH ROOKE	H	M	08JUN1697	TOTNES			11JUN1980IF	M051751	2464
LAVERS, WILLIAM	ROBERT LAVERS/	M	C	03DEC1699	BERRY POMEROY	19MAR1974OG	07MAY1974OG	24MAY1974OG	C050291	1858
LAVERS, WILLIAM	HENRY LAVERS/	M	C	13FEB1703	BUCKFASTLEIGH	CHILD	CHILD	08OCT1974PV	C050031	3368
LAVERS, WILLIAM	HENRY LAVERS/	M	C	01AUG1708	BUCKFASTLEIGH	14JUN1974PV	10SEP1974PV	08OCT1974PV	C050031	3548
LAVERS, WILLIAM	MARY GILDRON	H	M	04OCT1713	BUCKFASTLEIGH			13DEC1977LA	M050031	0957
LAVERS, WILLIAM	CHRISTOPHER LAVERS/JOAN	M	B	20JAN1715	YEALMPTON	12JUL1973LG	10NOV1973LG	16NOV1973LG	7301726	38
LAVERS, WILLIAM	MARY HODGE	H	M	05SEP1718	MALBOROUGH			30OCT1978SL	M051341	1547
LAVERS, WILLIAM	WILLIAM LAVERS/MARY	M	C	01SEP1719	MALBOROUGH	09NOV1974PV	14JAN1975PV	11FEB1975PV	C051341	5552
LAVERS, WILLIAM		M	C	25JAN1722	PLYMPTON ERLE	31MAY1975LA	02JUL1975LA		C051521	1626
LAVERS, WILLIAM	MARY FRINCH OR FINCKE	H	M	11NOV1723	ASHBURTON			05SEP1978SL	M050201	1419
LAVERS, WILLIAM	RICHARD LAVERS/ELIZ	M	C	28APR1730	SLAPTON	01OCT1974LG	18JAN1975LG	12FEB1975LG	C052001	1695
LAVERS, WILLIAM	SUSANNAH DURANT	H	M	02APR1732	SLAPTON			28NOV1978SL	M052001	0554
LAVERS, WILLIAM	HENRY LAVERS/	M	C	03APR1745	TOTNES	12DEC1975SG	24MAR1976SG	26MAR1976SG	C051751	12558
LAVERIS, WILLIAM	JOHN LAVERIS/ELIZ	M	C	15DEC1751	SLAPTON	01OCT1974LG	25JAN1975LG	12FEB1975LG	C052001	1919
LAVERS, WILLIAM	RICHARD LAVERS/MARY	M	C	29AUG1756	PLYMPTON ERLE	31MAY1975LA	05JUL1975LA	29JUL1975LA	C051521	1968
LAVERS, WILLIAM	JOHN LAVERS/MARY	M	B	16SEP1764	YEALMPTON	12JUL1973LG	10NOV1973LG	16NOV1973LG	7301726	32
LAVERS, WILLIAM	THOMAS LAVERS/MARGERY	M	B	30JUN1765	YEALMPTON	04JAN1963	02MAR1963LA	16NOV1973LG	7301726	32
LAVERS, WILLIAM @	THOMAS LAVERS/MARGERY HINGSTON	M	B	30JUN1765	YEALMPTON	04JAN1963LA	02MAR1963LA	PRE-1970	0452926	FILM
LAVERS, WILLIAM	ELIZABETH STONE	H	M	20JAN1767	SLAPTON			28NOV1978SL	M052001	0618
LAVERS, WILLIAM	MARY SHAPCOTT	H	M	03MAR1768	EXETER, SAINT MARY STEPS			09MAR1978SG	M051011	0838
LAVERS, WILLIAM	WILLIAM LAVERS/MARY	M	C	10AUG1768	EXETER, SAINT EDMUNDS	CHILD	CHILD	17JAN1975IF	C050921	4863
LAVERS, WILLIAM	WILLIAM LAVERS/MARY	M	C	05JUN1773	EXETER, SAINT EDMUNDS	20AUG1974IF	11JAN1975IF	17JAN1975IF	C050921	5009
LAVERS, WILLIAM	RALPH LAVERS/MARY	M	C	26APR1774	AYLESBEARE	02MAY1974IF	16AUG1974IF	21AUG1974IF	C050261	2174
LAVERS, WILLIAM	JOHN LAVERS/JOAN	M	C	28SEP1777	UGBOROUGH	13DEC1975OG	20JAN1976OG	28FEB1976OG	C051771	8343
LAVERS, WILLIAM	JOHN LAVERS/MARY	M	C	14OCT1781	KINGSBRIDGE	30NOV1963LA	22FEB1964LA	28FEB1968SL	P001881	2981
LAVERS, WILLIAM	MARY REVEL	H	M	29DEC1785	HOLBETON			23JAN1964LA	A458470	0604
LAVERS, WILLIAM	RICHARD LAVERS/ELIZ	M	C	23APR1786	UGBOROUGH	13DEC1975OG	20JAN1976OG	28FEB1976OG	C051771	8627
LAVERS, WILLIAM	MARY LIGHT	H	M	30MAY1791	BRIXTON			19NOV1973LG	7301727	71
LAVARS, WILLIAM	JOAN CERBY	H	M	21OCT1794	EAST STONEHOUSE, SAINT GEORGE			15NOV1985SL	M150701	2114
LAVERS, WILLIAM	PHILIP LAVERS/MARY	M	C	16OCT1795	UGBOROUGH	16DEC1975OG	20JAN1976OG	28FEB1976OG	C051771	8978
LAVERS, WILLIAM	JOHN LAVERS/JENNY	M	C	13JAN1796	YEALMPTON	28SEP1974LA	09JAN1975LA	16JAN1975LA	C052221	4557
LAVERS, WILLIAM	JOHN LAVERS/SARAH	M	C	05FEB1796	UGBOROUGH	16DEC1975OG	20JAN1976OG	28FEB1976OG	C051771	8989
LAVERS, WILLIAM	RICHARD LAVERS/ELIZTH	M	C	18DEC1796	MODBURY	10SEP1974PV	02NOV1974PV	05DEC1974PV	C051461	10248
LAVERS, WILLIAM @	WILLIAM LAVERS/MARY REVEL	M	B	29OCT1804	HOLBETON	04JAN1963LA	02MAR1963LA	PRE-1970	0452926	FILM
LAVERS, WILLIAM	WILLIAM LAVERS/CRISTIN	M	C	04JUL1806	UGBOROUGH	16DEC1975OG	20JAN1976OG	02MAR1976OG	C051771	9352

Δ= ENTRY ALTERED FROM SOURCE; $,@,>=RELATIVES NAMED IN SOURCE. SEE "SYMBOLS" IN INSTRUCTIONS.

A = ADULT CHRISTENING B = BIRTH C = CHRISTENING D = DEATH OR BURIAL ALL OTHERS = MISCELLANEOUS
F = BIRTH OR CHRISTENING OF FIRST KNOWN CHILD M = MARRIAGE N= CENSUS W = WILL

A page of an IGI Microfiche

N census

S miscellaneous

W will or probate

There may be other symbols, some given at the bottom of each page. The rest are in the *Introduction to the IGI.*

The date of the event is in the next column. The period covered by the IGI is, with some exceptions, 1538–1875, with most entries in the 18th century.

The next column gives the place, generally the town and/or parish.

This completes the information generally required by the searcher. There are, however, another 5 columns:

B, E and S are relevant only to the members of the LDS Church. If they show *Infant* or *child*, the child died before reaching 8 years.

SOURCE-BATCH are the headings for the others. If these columns contain only numbers, the information has been submitted by a genealogist and more information can be obtained by writing to Salt Lake City, and paying a nominal fee for the postage and photocopying of the entire information.

For example '8421936' has the following meaning: 84 = 1984; 219 = day of the year (= 6th of August); 36 is the identification number of the submission.

If there are also letters given, then the information has been found in a register. One needs to add to that information the number of the 'Serial Sheet', which is the number in the last column, if more information is to be requested from Salt Lake City. It must, however, be noted, that this is not a free service and a fee is to be paid for the dispatch (largely the cost of the postage) of the relevant microfilm to the nearest LDS Genealogical Library, where the film can be consulted for a given period. There are people who, for a fee, will undertake research there on behalf of others. Many Americans go there during their holidays and, increasingly, so do English people as well as people of other nationalities. All are full of praise for what they find.

There is a very good article on the IGI, giving further details, in the FTM of October 1988, on pages 27 and 28, and April 1994 pages 21 and 22, and continued in the May issue on pages 14 and 15.

RELIABILITY OF THE IGI

Nothing on this earth is perfect. It was explained in the beginning of this topic, how carefully the lists are established. If one keeps in mind that no record is better than the original informant, and that computers can go wrong at times, then the IGI is as faultless as one can hope for.

It has already been stated, that each new edition builds on the previous one, which makes the search of previous editions unnecessary. This will be so, except when rare computer errors occur and some information is omitted, or entries based on personal information are removed for specific reasons.

LIMITATIONS OF THE IGI

One tends to despair when the entry looked for cannot be found. This does not mean the event has not taken place. Most likely, the event has not yet been put into the index and it is therefore important to remember that the index is not yet complete.

Add to this that people did move about, at least into nearby parishes and counties, and that parents were not very inventive with christian names; for instance, in the 18th and 19th centuries, names like Thomas, John, James, Mary and Elizabeth abounded, to name but a few.

Even today, children are named after a grandparent, a favoured relative or friend. Look at the following scenario:

Two brothers, Thomas and a much younger James (1), who has a wife Mary (1), both have several children. Thomas has a first-born, James (2).

You have found, in the parish, an ancestor called James, son of James and Mary. You find the marriage entry of James (1) and Mary (1) in the same parish and no other of the right names at the right time. You conclude that James (1) and his bride Mary (1)are your ancestors. However, you ignore the existence of James (2), son of Thomas, who also married a Mary, but in another parish that has not yet been indexed. He was, in fact, the father of your James. You can argue that this limitation would equally apply had you searched the original marriage registers only, and you are right. It is here that the building up of the 'lateral tree' is helpful, whereby you make the tree of the offspring of all ancestors, as they are found. Working from the past to the present is much more difficult, than the other way round.

In conclusion, use the IGI as a research tool only, and it will be of great help. The information found needs to be checked against the original entries and cross-referenced from other sources. For this purpose, 'link documents' are essential. Such a document, in the circumstances quoted above and referring to the ancestor, James, would establish the maiden name of his mother. Good examples of link documents are wills, particularly from well-to-do-maiden aunts, but also from grandparents who leave heirlooms directly to their grandchildren. Census returns and the like are also helpful in this way.

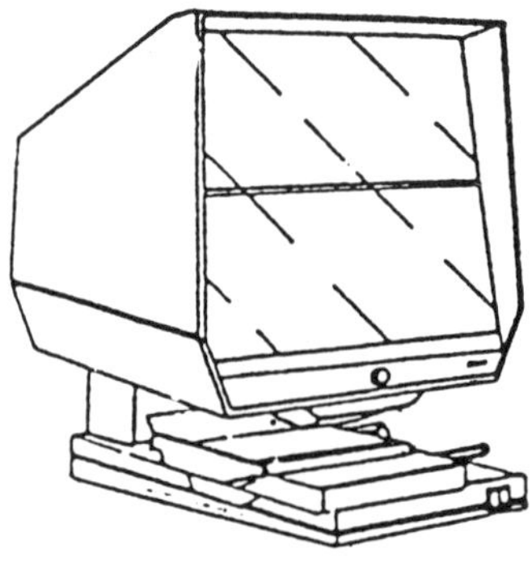

A typical Microfiche Reader

OTHER INDEXES

CARD INDEXES

These are very useful, as a personal research aid, even though you may have a computer. The card indexes are made with 'slips' of strong paper or library index cards, which withstand sorting much better. They are uniformly 5 x 3 inches (12 1/2 cm x 7 1/2 cm) and new entries are 'slipped in'.

MY OWN INDEX

Each card gives me, in the left top corner, the family name. Below this is the given name, and then the dates of the birth and death and the name of spouse, if they are known. In the right upper corner goes the place, and, below it, the year(s). On the lower part goes the type of information I have, details about where I keep it and where it was found, and the name of the researcher.

Luscombe — Devon
Thomasina — 1720
c:?

see also Eliza Luscombe
mentioned in will of
Walter Sorell (letter 12/5/89)
WDRO Card Index

researched by
Mary F.

Mary, the researcher, is a friend, and WDRO is in Coxside, Plymouth. When, in my researches, I come across Luscombe or Sorell (Walter Sorell also has a slip, although Mary does not yet know where he fits in), I am unlikely to remember anything specific; so I consult my index and write to Mary, if it concerns her. She does the same for me. The persons of our own tree are all on the computer index, by name and with a reference number, as explained in the section 'Numbering Ancestors'.

I have another index for source material, with several headings:

- 'Census' giving all the copies made and where filed.
- 'Directories' name, year, names on photocopy, first and last, and where filed.
- 'IGI' printouts, year, place, names and where filed.
- 'Leaseholds' Property, year, tenants/owners, where filed.
- 'Maps' area, if parish, tithe, ordnance, etc.
- Type of record, period, number and page of notebook where copy was entered.

LIBRARY CARD INDEXES

A great number of libraries have them, and they should be consulted carefully. It must be remembered, however, that the compiling of them has often taken many years of work and *cards must not be removed*. The public has access to them on trust, but I have seen a case where all the slips for one name were removed by a selfish researcher, with the result that now not even handbags are allowed into the library and must be left in lockers. Unless all users cooperate, access to these indexes could eventually be denied to the public, and made available only through staff and against a fee.

The most cited card index is the one of the Society of Genealogists in London. Few realise that there are other important local collections, such as those of Devon, one of which is in the West Country's Study Library, Exeter, in the same building as the CRO.

The SAGHS has many cupboards full of trays, holding a variety of card indexes. The most important refers to cemetery records; there are others, such as the Adelaide Hospital Admission Register, the Blair Newspaper Index (mainly 1862 - 1899), the Certificate Index, Destitute Index, School Admission and many more, all listed in the Library Guide. The collection is growing continuously, particularly for material for which the microfilming of records is not feasible. Others may be found in the Mortlock Library, on North Terrace, Adelaide.

STRAYS INDEX

An index of this kind is kept by all FHSs belonging to the Federation. Anyone finding an entry for a person who was not born in the area in which the event took place - be it marriage, death or whatever - is asked to make 2 slips, similar to the one shown above. It should give all the details of the event; e.g. a copy of the obituary, giving the exact source. Assume that you go to a Hong Kong cemetery and happen to notice the grave of a soldier belonging to a Devon Regiment. You might wish to copy all you can read on the gravestone, together with the name (and location) of the graveyard. Write up, once you are at home, a slip that would hold this information. Make a (carbon) copy. Here, you have a Briton who died overseas; so you then send the slips to the holder of the following card index.

BRITONS WHO DIED ABROAD

He is Mr D. H. Pearce, Wayside, Roman Road, Twyford, Winchester, Hants S021 1QW, England. He keeps one copy for his own index and sends the other one on to the Devon FHS or the 'Clearing House' for transmission, so that descendants of the relatives of that soldier can find the information in the Devon Strays Index. Mr Pearce also holds a card index for BRITONS WHO LIVED ABROAD, and he answers queries for a modest fee (3 IRCs or £1 for a single name and £5 for a full search for a given surname) from the information he has been gathering since long before he retired.

For those who are searching in England and who are able to go to London, The Society of Genealogists, 14 Charterhouse Building, Goswell Road, London EC1M 7BA, could be a starting point. One needs to be a member or pay a search fee. To take advantage of all that is on offer there, one should previously study their pamphlet, 'Using the library of the SoG'. That may be on the shelves of your local FHS or can be obtained by sending a SAE and a small fee, from the Society itself.

ACCOMMODATION

It becomes increasingly widespread over the years, to offer accommodation to fellow researchers, as more and more family historians travel further and further afield to gather information about their ancestors.

Members of a local FHS report their willingness to offer shelter to members from afar, lodging them at an affordable price. Some advertise in the FTM. The advantage of this is, above all, that it creates opportunities to meet kindred spirits. The hosts may also act as guides to the visitors, who, in return, may not only provide a new stimulus to them, but also be able to help them in their research.

BIOGRAPHICAL REGISTERS

These indexes are increasingly produced in Australia. They list, often on a state-wide basis, names in alphabetical order, and provide considerable information: birth or baptism date; place of origin if it is known; marital status and name of spouse; the place and date of marriage; names of children; religion; name of the ship on which the person arrived; the date of arrival. Some give date of death and place of burial, residence, etc. They lay no claim to being complete, only that the information is based on formal documents. These books differ from publications of this type elsewhere, in that the qualification for being listed is simply to have been a citizen in the colony over the period stated on the cover. Social status or achievements are not considered. In other biographical dictionaries, people are described, often in great detail. Those works are generally found on the open shelves of Australian FHS libraries.

BIOGRAPHICAL DICTIONARIES

These generally cover people in the public eye:

- National Biography 1910–1970.
- Who's Who. Published annually since 1897 with 'regional editions'.
- Who Was Who? is an occasional companion to the above.
- Burke has produced various works but some pedigrees therein have been questioned.

Debrett's books may also be found on library shelves.

There are others, covering various sections of the community, such as certain professions.

SHIPPING LISTS

In Australia, these give information on ship, date and port of departure, and date of arrival, but not always the names of the passengers. They are increasingly indexed (often only typescript) being found in the State Reference Libraries relevant to the respective Ports, eg. Mortlock Library, Adelaide, South Australia as well as in the main FHS libraries. These institutions may also hold some shipping lists of other States. Maritime Museums should also be investigated, wherever they exist.

In England, documents related to ship passengers lists are found also in the PRO KEW (under Board of Transport - 'BT - outwards', leaflet 7).

Passport Registers (FO 610) (1795–1943) are in chronological order. It is essential to realise that passports were not obligatory before World War 1 (1914).

In the USA, passenger and immigration lists, indexes and bibliographies have been compiled by Mr P. W. Filby and published by Gale Research, Detroit. Mr Filby has written a number of other books helpful to genealogists. In North–America, one needs to remember that due to a multitude of local events, the movement of people across the border between Canada and the USA was great, and many who landed, as migrants, in one country moved into the other.

MICROFORMS

This name is applied to both microfiche and microfilm. They are used increasingly worldwide. They need less storage space and are thought to be more durable than paper records. Most societies have steadily increasing numbers of indexes and records on film and provide the necessary readers. Very often, they also have machines that enable the making of photocopies of pages from these films and fiches. However, there are film indexes which may not be photocopied, such as the St Catherine's Indexes (BDM of England and Wales), South Australian Catholic Records and the New South Wales and Victorian Registration indexes, among others. The IGI may be photocopied. A fee which is charged, for the service, covers the use of the equipment, which it is prudent to book. In the SAGHS, one can make a booking (for 30 minutes) in person or by phone. In special circumstances, visitors from the country may book longer periods than the stated 30 minutes, in advance; otherwise, extensions can only be given if there are no other bookings at that time. Bookings are required no more than a week prior to the visit.

HAS IT BEEN DONE BEFORE?

GUILD OF ONE NAME STUDIES – GOONS

For the beginner, it is important to find openings, and some are with those 'who have done it before'.

One way to reach them is to see if there is a 'One Name Study' group that researches the relevant name. Here again, it is a matter of participating in the two-way process of giving and taking.

A guild was formed, where people who held information concerning a single name (with more research than just their immediate family) would be prepared to make this information available to others interested in the same name. This grew rapidly into an organisation, where there are now several levels of registration, right up to those who have searched and collected most of the materials available on the name, and whose researches cover several hundred years. People who represent a one-name study make themselves available to answer every enquiry which is accompanied by an SAE, and are expected to have available, at least, all information concerning that name, which can be found at St Catherine's House. Contact points are published by the Guild, and increasing numbers of newsletters are being produced. There are well over 1000 name entries and the list is growing steadily. A 'Register of One Name Studies' can be posted to you for a few pounds sterling (depending on where you are). If your FHS does not have one or you are not able to visit there, look to the GRD.

Send correspondence to the Guild of One Name Studies, Box G. 14, Charterhouse Buildings, Goswell Road, London EC1M 7BA, England.

If you are not one of the fortunate ones, whose name is on their lists, there are other openings, which are detailed below.

DIRECTORIES

There are several types.

Genealogical Research Directories

The GRD is the largest one. It has been published annually since 1981 by Keith A. Johnson and Malcolm R. Sainty in Australia. Copies can be found in most Australian public libraries. Current and previous issues can be bought from Mr K. Johnson, 17 Mitchell Street, North Sydney NSW 2060, Australia, and from Mrs Elizabeth Simpson, 2 Stella Grove, Tollerton Notts, NG12 4EY, England. In addition, there are agents in such countries as Canada, New Zealand and the USA. There is a list of names researched (more than 10,000 in 1989 as well as in 1993), giving area and timespan and the number of a researcher. In another list, the numbers designating researchers are followed by their names and addresses. Subscriptions for the following year's edition close around November, for a delivery May/June. For a fixed fee, one can put in 15 names researched; more can be added for an extra payment. One then receives a free copy of the publication. Each year, different people are likely to subscribe. The directory contains an up-to-date list of over 500 major genealogical societies worldwide, articles and other information. It is truly an international publication, with extremely helpful articles. You would find in it, in particular years, articles like the following:

- 1985 – When you write to Germany
- 1986 – When you travel to Germany
- 1987 – When you write to France
- 1988 – When you write to Scotland
- 1989 – Genealogical research in the Netherlands
- 1990 – When you write to Ireland
- 1991 – How to make the most of the GRD
- 1992 – Researching in Italy.

Where back numbers are out of print, Mr Johnson may be able to send xerox copies of the articles.

The 'National Genealogical Directory' (NGD), a very good English directory, was published by Mr Burchal until 1986. Since 1987, it has been edited by Iris Louise Caley. The last issue appeared in 1993 and no others will be produced.

The British Isles Genealogical Register

In 1993, the FFHS began to collect forms which they had distributed through their affiliated societies, record offices and other institutions likely to be frequented by family historians (FTM, May 1993 pages 21 and 22). On them anyone who wished, could, for one pound sterling, submit 16 names – each variation having to be listed separately. The 'Place of Interest' could be any parish (in the specific county). The county code (for which the Chapman Code had been provided) was sought, and then the country – which could be 'all', in which case the whole country of Britain could be searched. Finally, the period of interest had to be stated.

The information received toward the end of the year has been computerised, and the results grouped by counties in which the names are being searched, copies were going to the respective FHSs. Overseas members and readers can submit forms and the booklets can be bought individually, the address of the persons to be contacted in each county are listed in the FTM Aug. 1994 issue p. 8 & 9 The article in the FTM, April 1993 issue, page 41, gives further details.

A word of warning: it is unwise to search all through the country, unless a very rare name is involved, and all other avenues have been exhausted. I found that people who looked for 'all' references, for a fairly common name, were either unaware of what they were doing, or were collecting all the information with a view to compiling a one - name study. The reader, not being able to decide between the two motives, might not be willing to spend double postage or sending masses of information. The searcher might find the requested task greater than anticipated, and answer selectively, thereby causing displeasure. I keep a mailing list, and people who do not respond are not contacted again. I know I am not alone in this practice; even

Mr Camp, Director of the SoG London, commented once on having suffered such treatment.

There are others, less important works, and it pays to check all sources which one finds.

Most of them use county abbreviations for England according to 'The Chapman County & Country Codes' (pre - 1974 counties), given in Appendix 1. The problem with modern England is that boundaries have changed several times. New 'counties' have been formed, such as Avon (Bristol Area) and Humberside (Hull Area). For Avon, Gloucester should be searched first, and later Wiltshire and Somerset. For Humberside, check first in South Yorkshire, and then in Lincolnshire, unless the location of the township is already known.

Directories Of Member's Interest

These are published by most Family History Societies, either separately every few years or in their quarterly journals. As these societies exchange their publications with other members of the FFHS, you are likely to have access to the majority of these directories in your FHS library. A good idea is to become a member of the local society of the area in which you are researching. The list of addresses can also be obtained from the FFHS.

RESEARCH BY CORRESPONDENCE

When the relevant Record Office or depositories of documents cannot be visited, correspondence becomes a way of researching.

This can be done by employing either a genealogist or a record agent. One way of finding such a person is to contact AGRA, which stands for the Association of Genealogists and Record Agents. It was founded in 1968, to protect both members and clients, and prides itself on maintaining the high standards of its members. The contact address of the AGRA is The Secretary, 29 Badgers Close, Horsham, W. Sussex RH12 5RU. From there, the addresses of its members can be obtained for one pound fifty pence sterling, or for five IRCs This list can also be bought at the SoG, PRO and Guild Hall Library, all in London.An alternative is to look to journals in your FHS Library, including the Family Tree Magazine, for advertisements. Some FHSs provide a search service within their own holdings.

Whatever you do, if you want an answer, you must send an SAE or IRCs. The postage, particularly overseas, is a burden that no institution or business can bear any longer, let alone a private individual you may address for help. The latter must be at least re-imbursed for expenditure that he or she has made on your behalf, and generally this should be dealt with in advance.

On the other hand, if you place a notice in a publication, and expect some correspondence in return, you must answer each reply, even if the message is of no interest whatsoever to you.

The cost of the IRCs is prohibitive, but, as one of them will only cover a letter of minimum weight, by sea, in order to avoid delays of up to three months for delivery, it is necessary to send, at the very least, two IRCs. The Post Office explains that the high cost is justified, because people used to buy IRCs in quantities in place of money orders to transfer money, their price has to be equitable with the high fees for international bank-cheques. One way around this expense is to buy stamps from a stamp dealer. Your post office should have information on current rates in foreign countries, although I have not always found this to be the case. You need to do some intelligent guessing. based on the official rate of exchange. A warning needs to be sounded about international postage, currently German postage for letters is more than double the Australian rate, which in turn exceeds that of the UK rates. If you tell the dealer why you require the stamps and accept his advice, you may save money. One can buy, from the FTM, stamps for England, Canada, New Zealand, USA and South Africa. To this last country, only stamps should be sent, although IRCs may have been made valid again. The instructions and exchange rates are found on the contents page of the FTM. I do not avoid IRCs altogether, and you may need them for the Channel Islands, Isle of Man and Ireland, as English stamps are not valid there. Family members might be glad to send stamps as gifts, or travelling friends may buy them on your behalf.

Suggestions about finding correspondents have already been given under the headings of 'Has it been done before?', and more can be found in FTM under 'Readers Interests' and 'Connections Sought'.

Your finding a person who is researching your name, in your locality and at your time, is a find indeed, as you will be able to join forces in your search. Many distant (and not so distant) cousins have been found in this way.

In opening communication with a fellow researcher, it is suggested that a first letter should be sent only to establish contact, so that no valuable material is lost. I have been told that some people make a point of telephoning first, and then confirming their interest by letter. When an answer is received, it is courteous to thank the correspondent. I have found that this action has positive results, and I have received newly discovered information much later, without even asking for it. I have also found that, if I can do research in exchange for work done graciously for me elsewhere, then the repayment of postage is dropped; this arrangement of mutual help is definitely the most satisfying way of researching if travelling is not possible.

The interest of the receiver of a letter needs to be awakened and maintained. The pattern of successful letters in genealogy is similar to that of a business letter. It must be short - one page maximum - and yet contain all the relevant information that will be helpful to the recipient. Extra information can be given by adding a 'fact sheet' to your letter, which would contain all the detailed relevant information in a well displayed way; it might be part of the tree centering on the person being studied or table of chronological events; but too much text should be avoided. As display is important, use your artistic flair. Imagine what you would like to receive, when dealing with such letters all day, every day. Make a draft and then use the following checklist of the items your letter should contain:

- Your name, postal address (printed)
- date
- name and address of recipient
- statement of your purpose in the first paragraph
- a proper display of the details of the person being researched;

  JOHN ALLEN

  married around 1860

  ELIZA (BATT??)

  suspected area: Tunbridge Wells, Kent.
- the name, date and place of the subject searched.
- a brief statement of other relevant facts.

  eg. their daughter, Eliza Batt Allen, was baptised around 1861 in Tunbridge Wells.
- a courteous, considerate tone.
- correct facts (figures are easily transposed. 1861 becoming 1816, etc.)
- dates of any other person of the same name.
- clear and concise text, check long sentences, in particular.
- the completeness of the information.
- any offer of help which you can make.

When writing your final letter ensure that you

- make a copy for your file.
- check that all can be read easily (print names).
- enclose a stamped, self-addressed envelope.
- see that the envelope is properly addressed.

Whenever possible, check the address in the latest telephone book – if your correspondent has recently changed address, the Post Office is likely to know and forward the mail.

Put your full address on the back, under 'sender', so that the letter can be returned to you if for any reason it does not reach its destination.

Addresses change frequently. If the required telephone book is not available, the latest GRD in your local library should be consulted. Otherwise, the librarian may have the latest relevant almanacs. If that fails, the State (County) Reference Library should have a recent publication with the address you seek, but only for institutions and societies.

Above all, be patient. I wrote a letter to a person, seeking a specific record to be searched. As the offer sounded as if the only cost would be out of pocket expenses, I stated that I would cover these. Six months later I had heard nothing. I received another offer, but feared that I would get two answers both requesting expenses. So I wrote a second letter to the first correspondent asking for a prompt answer. Six weeks later, a most apologetic letter came: my first request had never arrived, while my second had been mislaid and had just been found. He would now 'just get on with it' and not ask for prepaid expenses.

From this it is clear how important it is to fix fees before any work is started. A photocopying fee of 20p per sheet can blow out easily to 20 pounds, when PRO handling fees and airmail postage are added to a number of large documents which may all be included in apparently single referenced files.

ELUSIVE BDMs

and how to find them

It looks so simple: just take the indexes of the birth and marriage registers and work backwards. This may be the case when your ancestors did not change their place of residence, generation after generation, or your ancestors owned their land and handed it down your ancestral line. Most people are not so fortunate.

The first record of an ancestor that is found is on the birth entry of that person's child. In recent times, both parents are named, and the mother's maiden name is given. However as you go back in time, you are likely to find only her first given name. Sometimes her first and second Christian names appear but not her maiden name. If the IGI is used, you have the advantage of being given other parishes of the county, but have the disadvantage of the index being very incomplete. Nevertheless, it is a good starting point. Extract all siblings of the ancestor whom you know, who were born to the same parents in the same parish. Make them into a chronological tree:

PARISH A

William Tree = Charity

1776	1778	1780	1784	1786	1790
William	John	Mary	Thomas	Samuel	John

It is likely that those under your consideration are offspring of the same couple, but you cannot be certain, as there are quite a few families surnamed Tree in the parish register. However, Charity does seem to be an unusual name in this parish at that time. You conclude they had 6 children over 14 years; so they were most likely married. Finding nothing in the parish marriage register for 1775, you work backwards for 10 years. Still nothing. You suspect they might have left it late to marry and search up to 1790 – still nothing. So, you conclude that William married Charity in her parents' parish which was elsewhere; so back you go to the IGI.

PARISH B

LOOKING FOR PARISH BOUNDARIES

Could this be the same couple? The dates fit, but you are still not sure. You consult a map giving parish boundaries and see that the two parishes lie next to each other. You look for taxes paid by William Tree (these were pre-census days) and start with the Tithe Apportionments which have been transferred from the Parish Chest A to the County Record Office. They have survived and you find there was only one William Tree who paid this tax from 1779 to 1810. You note the location and see the tithe had been paid before 1779 by a Thomas Tree. Next you request the Ordnance Map, look for the location and find that there is a small river flowing not far from the church. You realise that your ancestors needed to cross a bridge to go to church. Then you read, in the local history book, that the little river was not only in flood after heavy rains in Spring 1782, but that the wooden bridge next to the church was so badly damaged, that it was replaced by one of stone, which you have already seen. This makes it likely that the Tree family decided that the Parish Church B was more convenient. What happened in 1788 is still to be detected. You have not yet established for certain if this is the same family, nor are you closer to pinpointing the marriage of the parents. Back to the IGI.

PARISH C

You find only one baptismal entry for Thomas Tree, baptised in 1774, to William and Charity Tree.

Had Charity gone home to her mother to have her first child? If so, she might have been born there. The Parish Registers are elsewhere, but the BTs are available. You find a Charity Roberts married to William Tree in 1773, as well as a Charity Roberts baptised in 1750. This looks promising. As this Parish is over 15 miles from Parish A , you might have two different couples. However, when looking at the Banns Book of Parish A, you find that for three weeks, in April 1773, the banns were read for William Tree of this Parish and Charity Roberts of Parish C. You search the marriage entry and learn that the groom was 'of age'. Theoretically, that means he was over 21, although this was not always the case, but with a bride of 24, he would be likely to be between 20 to 29 years old. You will find him, born in 1746, first born son of Thomas and Mary Tree, of that parish. His god-mother was Elizabeth Tree.

Generally, you can guess that a husband is 24 - 29 years old, when he marries for the first time.

In the burial register of parish A, the entry for Thomas Tree, aged 2, son of William and Charity, is found in the 1776 records.

If you are in luck, you will find a will of Elizabeth Tree, spinster, sister of Thomas Tree, who died in 1790, aged 70, who left her silk petticoats to her dear niece Mary, and the brooch she got from her mother, to her beloved niece, Elizabeth Tree.

A major stumbling block to accurate research may be a change in the spelling of a surname of an ancestral line. This can be slight or quite extreme. For instance, most vowels in a name could be altered and some consonants could be altered or dropped, H being the most notable. A person who could not write and who moved to an area where a different dialect was spoken, was the most exposed to an alteration of the surname. If one adds to this the complication of clerks who were hard of hearing, or who had their own styles of writing, or whose education was only partial or who thought that they had superior knowledge, then the possibility of variations increases markedly.

Standardisation of names began in the first part of the 18th century, coinciding with the appearance of the first dictionaries. For instance, it took careful examination to notice that the name 'Courtice' was spelt consistently in a Devon parish register until 8th March 1764. From its next appearance in October of the same year, it was 'Courtis'. Soon after this, a doting maternal grandfather of a different dialect transformed it into 'Courtes', to be handed down as a second Christian name, through the generations, to this day.

You need to be a detective, looking for clues, searching for further evidence but, above all, you must not jump to conclusions. Investigate all sources you can possibly find. Base your findings only on well documented facts. Be always critical of information found, particularly if it is not consistant, and evaluate your evidence, a process which will be discussed later.

DEATHS – BURIALS – MONUMENTAL INSCRIPTIONS

Most people tend to ignore the later years of their ancestors lives, which is sad, because, quite often, much can be learned from the information surrounding them.

One never knows how long one's ancestors lived, unless one engages in much searching in other sources. The IGI includes details of death only in the exceptional circumstances, when the babe died before baptism. Even such an event as this was not always recorded in the parish register, as the entry involved a fee.

If an approximate date of death is known, local newspapers are good places to search. Legal notices contain advertisements, placed by trustees and solicitors concerning deceased estates, so that creditors, beneficiaries and people who have claims against the estate can present their cases, for payment of outstanding debts. Debtors are also expected to pay their dues before a given date. Most wills pass probate within a year or two. However, I have come across two exceptions. An 'Administration with will of goods' was granted in August 1804, re-granted in December 1816 and for a third time in January 1838. After this, no further entry could be found, nor the grant of the corresponding probate. In another instance, a widow died intestate in November 1977, and her estate was settled in July 1992 – it took nearly 15 years.

Names of the trustee companies and solicitors can be found in directories such as the Yellow Pages. The more important ones in South Australia are the Public Trustee, Farmers Co-operative Executors and Trustees Ltd that became IOOF Australia Trustees Ltd; whilst the Executor Trustee Australia Ltd and Elder Trustee Executors Ltd are now incorporated into Austrust & Executor Trustee. However, a search involving them can be complex and time consuming, particularly if the exact date and/or place of death is unknown.

Death records for more recent times can be found in the relevant registers, established by the State, in the country in which the deaths occurred. Entries for Britons who died abroad may be found in the countries where they died, or in the Consular Returns (since 1849) in St Catherine's House. I know of a case, where husband and wife, both English - born, died within months of each other, abroad. The details for the husband could be found only in the Consular Returns whilst those for his wife were recorded only in the local death register and in her obituary in the local daily paper.

Burials are registered in the parish to which the cemetery belongs and/or by the cemetery authorities.

For earlier times, the parish burial registers need to be consulted, as well as the Bishop's Transcripts. Gravestones can be searched for, but not all have survived and, in some areas, the stones have been removed. Generally, attempts have been made to keep records of the inscriptions, before they have been destroyed or used in churchyard walls or laid as paving stones,where use and weathering hastens the erosion of the inscriptions.

After their foundations, the first task many family history societies started was the registration of MIs, which stands for Monumental Inscriptions, mostly from gravestones. Before that, only noteworthy cathedrals had this done by researchers; there is, for example, *The Roll Call of Westminster Abbey*, by E. T. Murray Smith (London 1912). Quite a few who search this book may find that they are descendants of someone listed there. If your ancestor was an important member of the community, the grave might well be inside the village church, or have its stone embedded in the wall, inside or out, or in the row of VIPs, close by. Vandalism is not new, old stones have also eroded, depending on material, time and exposure. I found recently one stone just over 50 years old, and photographed it. I was glad I had copied out the text, which is not clear in the photograph, as letters had fallen off. Even while copying from the stone, itself, we had to look closely to ensure we had the text right. Older stones are often overgrown, and need coaxing to reveal their information. The scrubbing brush is often insufficient; so talcum powder and different angles of light are used. The list of methods is never ending and the volunteers are worthy of the grateful thanks of all who benefit from their labours.

On the gravestones, one often finds, besides the name the date of burial or death, the age or even the birth date. Very often, there are other members of the family buried nearby, or who are remembered as fallen in war and buried elsewhere. Sometimes, an entire family over two and three generations can be found. The age given must be used with great care, as it can be misleading. The crassest error which I discovered, related to a boy, who died when 10 years old, in 1842. I knew this as fact, as I had found his obituary in two local newspapers and his death notice inserted by his grieving parents. The MI gave the right date of death but the age recorded was 70 years. Obviously, over 130 years after the event, the figure '1' of the '10' had eroded and was interpreted to have originally been a 7, not a 1. The information, 'son of...', made it quite clear that this was the person being researched and not somebody else with the same unusual name. The problem becomes aggravated when the name is more common. In most cases, the information is accurate and can lead to the finding of the birth certificate, and sometimes even to a marriage entry ('wife of 30 years').

WILLS, ADMONS, PROBATE, INVENTORIES

To family historians, wills are as useful as they are neglected. This is, however, understandable. Long ago, it is estimated, only 10% of the population made wills - women only if they were widows or spinsters, with property to leave. The will was often made on the deathbed, or not long before death. In contrast, well - planned wills were in the hands of solicitors, often made executors, or co-executors with the surviving spouse. If the estate did not call for deathduty, the will was generally not registered by a court; it stayed with the solicitor until his firm was dissolved or sold, or until it ran out of space. Some were sold to 'antiquarian' collectors, and occasionally you hear outcries from people who find them in second-hand bookshops. Sometimes they are bought by institutions, increasingly by record offices, local libraries and individuals who attempt to make them available to descendants.

The situation is different when the estate requires the payment of death duties, or when a person with property dies intestate (having made no will). Then the court must be advised.

In the first case, the executor must compile an inventory, which establishes the extent of the deceased estate, and evaluate it. In the second case, the court appoints an administrator to perform the functions of an executor (hence Administration - Admons). The executor/administrator asks for probate at the local court, which assesses the death duty to be paid; once this is done, probate is granted and the estate is distributed according to the will or the laws of intestacy.

In a search for a will of recent date, the first step is to find the Probate Registry of the local court. For instance there is only one Probate Registry for the State of South Australia, which is in the same building as the Supreme Court in Adelaide. The indexes, covering several years at a time, give name, date and place of death, as well as a reference. With this reference, one can order the will over the counter or, for an extra fee, it can be ordered by mail. The prices vary greatly, not only from country to country, but also from State to State, but wills are generally the cheapest personal documents to buy.

Some wills, or copies of them, are kept at Somerset House, London, but only if they passed probate after 11th January 1857. These are the wills of former residents of England or Wales, or of people who died abroad while owning property there. The indexes are alphabetically arranged for each year, and District Probate Registries (there are about 30 in England and Wales) may have a copy of these indexes. They may give much information: the name; the date and place of death; often the profession; the marital status - widow or spinster, in the case of women; the value of the estate; the place where the will was proved; and who swore the oath – generally the executor. Very often, this information may suffice, but wills can tell a great deal about the family and the ancestor's way of life. On the other hand, I have seen a will stating nothing but 'One half of my estate goes to my wife. The other half is divided between my two sons.' The executor was his friend, a lawyer, and nothing new was learned.

If the date of probate is known (in most cases within a year or two after death), one can write to the Chief Clerk, The Probate Sub-Registry, Duncombe Place, York YO1 2EA. Cheques are to be made out to H M Paymaster General and the non-refun-dable fee is two pounds for a simple will, which may involve a three-year search. Another copy is held at the registry where probate was granted. If this registry is known, the will may be bought there for a lesser sum than from Somerset House.

Wills before 1857 passed probate in ecclesiastical courts. Basically, wills were proven in the court under the jurisdiction of which the estate of the deceased was situated. If the deceased property was held in more than one See (Bishop's territory), then the Prerogative Court of York (PCY) was to grant probate for the estate in the province of York. Wills subject to this process can now be found in the Borthwick Library of the University of York. All the rest of the people of England and Wales, as well as Britons abroad, obtained probate from the Prerogative Court of Canterbury (PCC). Their wills are referred to as PCC wills and are in the PRO Chancery Lane, London, where indexes are arranged according to the year; there one can order the film on which a given will is photographed. There are viewers to enable reading of the film. One can also buy a photocopy of the will.

Calendars are indexes, often in chronological order, in which only the first letters are arranged alphabetically. They therefore take longer to search than an ordinary index.

To find a will in England, every possible court at which probate could have been granted must be searched, and this is quite intricate. J. S. W. Gibson's Guide, *Wills and where to find them* has been updated and retitled *Probate Jurisdictions: where to look for wills (4th Edit).*

If you know the year of death or probate, you may write to the PRO Chancery Lane, London WC2A 1LR, enclosing an SAE and details of what you are seeking; it is best to enquire for one will at a time, unless they are made in the same year. Ask whether it is there and enquire about the cost of the copy. You will need a cheque for the costs in pounds sterling, which will include postage (by sea, unless stated otherwise), packing and handling. If you know all the exact references of your requirements, you can order up to three wills; handling fees are £2.35 per item, but you save on postage.

INVENTORIES

These are not always kept with the wills and need to be searched for separately. One might begin a search by looking at 'Death Duties' at PRO Chancery Lane. I have found several in the State Government Archives of various countries.

SCOTTISH WILLS

Since the earlier part of the 19th century (1823) testaments and their indexes have been part of the Sheriff Court Records, and they are kept at the Scottish Record Office. Present day enquiries are dealt with at New Register House, in Edinburgh. The Scottish Record Society has published many indexes to wills submitted to the Commissary Court. The first of these is dated 1514.

There is no national index as such.

PROBATE IN THE USA

Probate records in the USA have always been under the jurisdiction of the civil government. They are filed in the county courthouse and kept either in the care of the clerk of the county court or of the county clerk. In some of the New England counties, State, town or district probate courts existed in early times. Probate records are still recorded on a town basis in Rhode Island, and on the basis of districts in Connecticut and Vermont.

CENSUS

The date of the first census - and its usefulness - varies from country to country. For instance, in New South Wales, Australia, the 1828 census is quite informative, as is the 1841 census of South Australia. The primary source documents for later ones are totally destroyed once the information needed is extracted. The compiled data can still be useful. If, for example, you know your ancestor lived in a small community in 1881, you can check the census for that year and look at the number of inhabitants in that particular village. If that number matches the number of people who could read and write in that community, you can assume that your ancestor possessed that skill.

Most countries apply the rule of privacy, and do not divulge any census information for 100 years. Sometimes exceptions are made, when a good case is put to the authorities, but one must either be a direct descendant of the subject of the enquiry, or have the written permission of a descendant to do the research. Then the information requested may be given; the census entry will not be produced.

Basically, the government of the day, to plan for the future, needs knowledge of the composition of the people it governs. Will there be more schools or larger poor houses required? Are there too many people crowded into small houses? Many types of other considerations prompt the questions in a census return. One consideration not taken into account is the curiosity of the descendants who want to learn about the lifestyles of their ancestors.

In England, census returns have been made every ten years, beginning with 1801; only 1941 was omitted, due to the war. Here, the '100 year rule' applies. In 1951, the 1851 census was made available to the public. It was the first released that is of real help to the family historian. The census of 1841 is of limited value, as it does not give as much helpful information and those between 1801 and 1831 are mostly useless, as the information cannot be linked to individuals, except in rare cases, like the set of data for St Clements, Hastings, for 1831. Before the 19th Century, similar lists were made, mostly at the parish level, and kept in the parish chest. If they survive, they may be in the same institution that holds the registers.

Areas were subdivided, and a census return collector was appointed. His task was to go from house to house, see that the returns were properly completed, collect them, collate them and return them to his supervisor. Imagine the scenario. In some places near the docks of London several families would live in quite small houses. Not all could read and write. Some did not know where they came from or when they were born. The Christian names given were often nick-names, different from those used in the birth register. Divorces may not have been common, but men walked out of families and started new ones, even bigamously, or changed their names and had no wish to be discovered. At the other end of the scale, the butler, filling in the names of the servants, was often satisfied to give the family name and status ('kitchen maid') and then guess at her age; the place of birth was only too easily overlooked. And not only the lady of the house may have been coy about her age. No wonder that these census collectors complained about their meagre pay, saying that they had been kept in the dark about all that was involved.

To find an ancestor in a census return is easy, if you know his exact address, but keep in mind that there might be complications. It might be that the collector did not follow the numerical order of a street, going first one side, and then the other. He might have missed houses because nobody was at home and then returned later. If the street was short, research should not be difficult. Beware, however, when a street was divided between two different districts. The pitfalls seem to be many, but the task is, increasingly, made easier by the work of the FHS, which provide the volunteers who index the census in their areas, in cooperation with the corresponding Record Offices. Depending on the cost of production, the printed indexes can be bought for a modest fee. They generally give the names of the families with the reference which enables the searcher to find the relevant census record. Most give only the name of the head of the household, and some an idea of the address or area. They vary but they are very helpful for those who do not know where to look first.

The census returns are the only documents to remain in Chancery Lane, at least for the time being. (No decision seems to have been made, as yet, over the future use of these buildings.)

The advantage of the census lies in giving a picture of the family at that time, and acting as a 'link-document'. Generally, children under ten years of age can be expected to be at home; from twelve years upwards, they could well be elsewhere in service, or be at boarding school. Other family members may be in hospital, in the army or even in gaol. If you suspect such a situation, look up the census for the relevant institutions. If you suspect that a death has occurred, search the death register or the MI, generally published by the local FHS. (They may have a card index that they will search for you.) You find this information in most English FHS journals, near their front or back covers. Others produce library guides every few years.

Census returns are often available locally, for example at the County Record Office, etc. The PRO in London, Chancery Lane has a complete set for England and Wales on microfilm. Previously, they were held in the Census Room of the nearby Land Registry Building, Portugal Street. This is the only part of the PRO to which a member of the public has access without holding a reader's ticket. Before visiting, be thoroughly prepared and be early to ensure that a film reader is available.

In England and Wales, you can expect to find the following information:

The census of 1841 gives the address, the name, the age, the occupation and states whether the person was born in that county by requesting a simple *yes or no* answer. The ages of adults is given 'to the nearest round figure'; those of children are meant to be accurate.

The returns from 1851 onwards provide the same details as above, but also the place of birth – at least the county. All ages are meant to be correct. Visitors recorded at the time of the census can provide valuable clues about family relations. Often, married daughters visited with their children, nieces and nephews were given shelter, etc. Also names of nearby households, familiar from the family tree, should be noted, as relatives often lived nearby.

In Scotland, the films can be seen in the New Register House, Edinburgh (GRO for Scotland).

In Ireland, the address is the Public Record Office Four Courts, Dublin 7. However, like a great deal of the Irish material, nearly all census returns of the 19th century have been destroyed. Those of 1901 and 1911 are already available.

The early census returns of the Isle of Man, 1821-1871 are on the Island, in the Manx Museum, and the National Trust, Douglas. The rest are in the PRO London, where all can been viewed on microfilm. The 100 year rule applies.

The Channel Islands returns are included in those of England and Wales.

There is a Gibson Guide (FFHS), *Census returns on microfilm*, showing where they can be found. The 1988 edition does not show the locations of the LDS Church Family History Centres. However, Mr Armstrong has composed such a list (FTM, May 1994, p 17 – 18). The 5th Edition of this Guide is called *'Marriage, Census and Other indexes for Family Historians'.*

There are three articles, by Tom Wood, on census returns, in the FTM issues of January, February and March 1994.

There is an 1881 Census Index of England and Wales, including the Channel Islands and Isle of Man. An article about that project can be found in the FTM of April 1991, pages 27 – 29.

Various parts of the world that were under British Administration produced very helpful census returns in 1828, giving name, age, marital status, occupation, the number of children that were alive at the time, and other information, depending on the area.

In the USA nationwide, censuses taken since 1790 (every 10

years) are available on microfilm all over America, and elsewhere through your nearest LDS library. (See chapter on IGI) They can be purchased for a few dollars.

Three catalogues can be obtained from the Publication Sales Branch, National Archives Trust Fund Board, Washington DC, USA, 20408:

- Federal Population Census 1780 - 1890.
- 1900 Federal Population Census
- 1910 Federal Population Census

Having studied the catalogue, one can then decide whether to buy the film, consult it in person where it is available, or employ someone to do the work.

Until 1840, only heads of households were listed along with the number of people to that household. The numbers of males and females were given separately, as were the numbers of free persons and slaves.

As from 1850, the American census lists all present with their full names, giving the states in which they were born, their ages and occupations, and the value of real estate owned. They show whether the person was illiterate, or attended a school during this year, or had married, or was physically handicapped. The information on real estate leads the researcher to the public lands records.

A commercial firm, called Accelerated Indexing Systems, has indexed all American Census Returns through to 1850, in printed volumes, one for each state.

Every census holds more information than the previous one. For instance, for1880, the place of birth is given, as well as the names of the parents of each person.

This census was indexed by the Federal Government for families having children ten years old or younger, as they often had no easy access to birth certificates, yet needed them to establish their age for social security payments.

Most of the 1890 census was lost in a fire, but the 1900 census tells us a great deal more, giving some insight into people's lives. It reveals whether each home was rented or owned as a freehold property or mortgaged. For immigrants, it shows the date of arrival in the USA, and indicates whether the head of the household was naturalised. (His wife and children were automatically given the same status.)

The 1920 Census is indexed like the one of 1900, the 1910 census being only partially indexed.

NEWSPAPERS AND GAZETTES

There is a wealth of information to be found in these publications. Personal notices of births, marriages, deaths and obituaries are those most sought.

Gazettes contain Government announcements but, particularly in earlier times, they could contain more about the average citizen than a list of bankruptcies. About 180 years ago, according to their family Bible, a child was born to English parents in Malta, then under British Administration. No formal records of the event were found. Then, a notice of an auction was discovered in the local Gazette, advising of an auction to be held for the sale of property belonging to the mother of the child, as the lady was leaving the island . For the researcher, this notice establishes her presence there at the relevant time.

To find such information is not easy, particularly, when the papers are not indexed. Fortunately, there are some that are indexed, and volunteers from FHSs help with this task, particularly in Australia. Much of *The Times* Newspaper (London) is not only indexed but on microfilm and can be consulted in some larger Public and University Libraries, worldwide. The same is true for the *Gentleman's Magazine*, which appeared first in 1731 and ceased publication in 1907.

The first place to look is the local newspaper office, if it was publishing at the relevant time. Then go to the local libraries, particularly for the Gazettes.

In England, a booklet, *Local Newspapers*, 1750 - 1920, compiled by J. S. W. Gibson and published by the FFHS, in 1987, shows, county by county, what newspapers were printed and where sets of them can be found. These sets are often incomplete.

Eve McLaughlin's Genealogical Guide, *Family History from Newspapers*, may also be of help.

In London, the best source is The British Library, Newspaper Library, Colindale Avenue, London NW9 5HE, telephone London 200 5515. It is opposite Colindale Tube Station (Northern Line).

To begin, consult the Catalogue of the British Library, Colindale, which should be available in most larger libraries. Before going to Colindale, establish contact, advising them what is needed, as information is not always up-to-date and sometimes whole years are missing, without this being mentioned in the catalogue. Much is on microfilm and a reader needs to be booked.

THE POOR AND OTHER PARISH RECORDS

Since 1601, the poor were the responsibility of the local parish, until being transferred in 1834 to 'Poor Law Unions' formed from groups of parishes. The poor were forbidden to beg. The records concerning them are of great value for the pre-census times, and particularly useful for 18th century England. They fall into two groups.

POOR RATE BOOKS

They concerned the ratepayers who lived in the parish and who paid taxes to support the poor. The entry gives generally not only the names, but also how much poor-rate was paid, the nature of their properties, and even their standing in society.

The other group of records dealt with the poor, themselves, and varied from parish to parish and between periods. Some of them are listed below:

WORKHOUSE INHABITANTS

Workhouse records listed the names of inmates, giving the dates of admission, and explaining when and why they left. Minute details about their physical condition may be found. Some had just fallen on hard times, due to illness, and others were quite destitute.

OUTDOOR RELIEF BOOKS

These books showed the monies paid to people who had their own homes but who needed help, people such as widows. At times, this assistance was suspended in the belief that it was more economical to have people in the workhouse. However, both forms of relief were available and were administered on the parish basis.

OVERSEER'S ACCOUNTS

These may have been kept separately or instead of the outdoor relief books.

Some parishes were richer than others. People, particularly workers in the field – often referred to as 'ag.lab' – moved from one place of employment to the next, trying to find shelter over those months when work was scarce. They soon became aware where better treatment could be obtained. The ratepayers, however, were not happy to support outsiders; so laws were passed by which a parish was entitled to reject the poor who were considered not to be their responsibility.

SETTLEMENT PAPERS

Poor persons who applied for relief from the parish had to establish their entitlement, that is, they had to be born in the parish to which they were applying. However, if an unmarried person had been working in the parish with an established parishioner for over a year, he generally was granted a settlement. If such a person fell on hard times, then the parish would help. The same could apply for a person who had arrived with substantial means.

REMOVAL ORDERS

These were issued when an application for settlement had not been granted, on the overseer's request, by two justices of the peace. The order enforced the return to the parish of birth, or of the last settlement granted. The Quarter Sessions provided the court to hear appeals against the removal order.

VESTRY MINUTES, CHURCHWARDEN AND CONSTABLE ACCOUNTS

These are other documents which hold information about those to whom monies were paid. In addition, they detail payments of rates, and other particulars of parishioners. In them, the word 'pass' meant that the person had to return to the previous parish.

These records were in use until the middle of the 19th century and constitute the reason why some ancestors have been accused of giving the wrong place of birth.

The researcher should remember that the baptism may have taken place in a parish different from the one of birth.

There were increasingly strict laws on vagrancy and their application is also recorded. Eventually, people could be shipped off, by parishes, to plantations in the colonies.

In England, you would find such records, which were originally kept in the parish chest, in the appropriate Record Office, generally the CRO. To give the location of known records, there are publications, such as *British Archives, A Guide to Archive Resources in the UK* by Foster and Sheppard. It is expensive to buy but may well be on your library's shelf. *The Parish Chest* by W. E. Tate is a valuable source of information on all these documents and should also be on the shelf. There is a concise account of these records in most large books on family history, including *Debrett's Family Historian* by Noel Currer-Briggs.

In Australia, the larger libraries of FHSs are likely to have card-indexes of the inhabitants of asylums and admission slips from public hospitals. Other information could be found in State archives, local archives, and Local History sections of the State Reference Libraries, such as the Mortlock Library in South Australia.

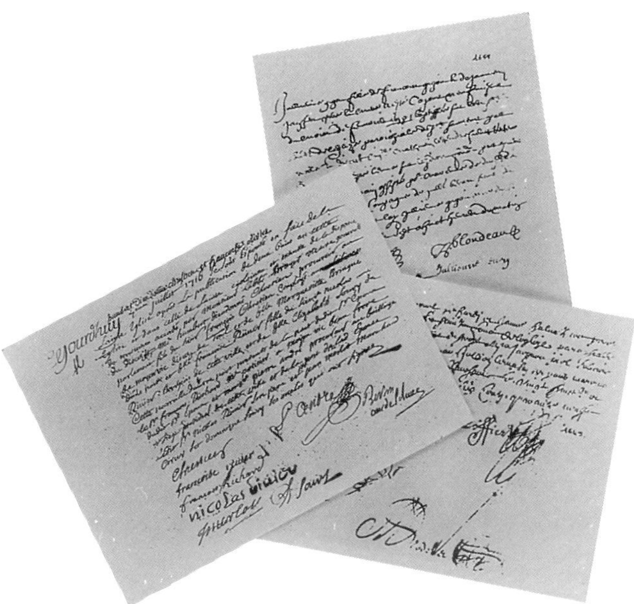

LAND TITLES AND DEEDS

Land can only change hands by a legal act or by inheritance.

Titles and deeds pertaining to land are often found to be of great assistance in tracing one's family.

AUSTRALIA

All land belonged originally to the Crown, which made grants to suitable citizens. Land can be leased and many of the pastoral properties are 'leaseholds'. Much is still Crown land today, for instance along waterways. The rest can be acquired as 'freehold' property. Each state holds the records of land ownership in its Department of Lands, in the Lands Titles Office. If one knows the location of the property in question, a search can be made at this department, against a fee. A land agent, broker or solicitor specialising in this field would know how to find a document as well as the relevant land tax records, faster than a layman.

USA

Lands records are varied. The Federal Government made grants to individuals, while bounty land warrants for un-allocated public land were commonly granted for military service. Apart from these, the National Archives hold various applications and private land claims, and can provide a list of professional record searchers.

Land grants made by the states are in the state archives or the county court house.

Deeds are records of transfer of land titles from one private individual to another and can be helpful by showing the previous address of the buyer and the new address of the seller, or of the heirs. If the land was held by several generations of the same family, the deed is likely to state that as well. A transfer may only be registered on the deed, a new deed not being necessary. The custodian of these registers of deeds is likely to be in the county court house; in New England, the town clerk should be approached.

SCOTLAND

Legal records, relating, in particular, to land ownership by acquisition or inheritance, are in the General Record Office.

The most important are testaments (wills), 'Service of Heirs' and deeds.

Testaments and 'Service of Heirs' can include much family information and can identify people who died intestate.

Deeds cover a wide range of agreements, such as bonds, sales and marriage contracts.

Sasines record the ownership of real estate, as well as the transfer of land and houses. They were in use before the 17th century.

The system was modified around 1847.

There have been, since 1855, valuation rolls, which detail both landlords and tenants, property by property throughout Scotland.

ENGLAND

In England, the situation is so complex that researchers have avoided using the sources available, which can date to the 11th century. Even today, the Church of England is one of the largest 'landlords' of the country, holding by grant, property from the Crown, who is the ultimate owner of all land. Landlords leased land by 'copyhold'. That means a deed (copied from the record of the Manor Court) was written out. It was also known as an indenture, because of the way it was made. It consisted of a T-shaped parchment. The deed was copied onto all three branches of the T, which would be cut by a wavy line (indenture). Each party in the agreement received half of the horizontal bar of the T, whilst the vertical bar was retained in the official records. These were called the 'Feet of Fines' and were like a modern record of payment. As the wavy lines of the 3 documents had to match up, the authenticity of the documents was ensured. Since 1922, copyhold has been finally abolished by law, and properties are now 'leasehold' and of limited duration, or 'freehold'. The latter can be either 'in fee simple', where the owner can dispose of it without restrictions, or 'in fee simple conditional', when ownership is restricted to a specific class of heirs and the property is said to be 'entailed'.

MANORIAL RECORDS

They had their origins in the 12th century, and it was only in 1977 that the Administration of Justice Act ruled that the manorial courts should cease to have jurisdiction to hear and determine legal proceedings. However, they could continue to do their other customary business.

The advantage of information from these rolls is that one can follow generations of ancestors who may have been tenants, and thus ensure that the information found in the parish registers actually refers to one ancestral line. It helps bridge missing entries, but must be used with care for that purpose, as there are pitfalls. Even if one does not need them to confirm a lineage, their information, concerning rents and the like, can throw interesting light on what the life of an ancestor might have been like.

For instance, one could find in the card-index of the WDRO the name of an ancestor, who had bought, in the middle of the 18th century, a lease from the estate of Sir John St Aubyn, Lord of the Manor of Stoke Damerel with a reference that leads to the record (rent book) that shows the address of the property leased, and the rental value, as well as the length of the lease. This is most important information. Because the 'three lives' of people given with their ages, that determine the length of the lease, are often heirs or close relatives of the leasees. Sometimes members of the Royal family are given as 'lives'. When the lease came closer to the end of 'its life', it could be re-negotiated, of course, against a fee, that also ensured a low rent. In more recent times, this might not have occurred in a session of the Manor Court, but in a solicitor's office, the 'three lives' being replaced by a fixed time, generally 99 years.

As from the administration of William the Conqueror, all lands belonged to the Crown and it was the King's prerogative to either keep the lands to himself and raise income from them directly, or to let others do it for him. In the first case, he appointed sheriffs, bailiffs or reeves to administer the lands on his behalf, taking himself the position of the Lord of the Manor. But mostly, he gave that role to his trusted friends, in return for their deeds on his behalf. Generally, a title went with the lands, called estates. However, these lords did not get their land for nothing; they had to pay rents to the King. Original rates were fixed in the famous Domesday Book of 1086 – nicknamed by some as 'Doomsday Book', because of the heavy payments involved. Added to this, the lords had to support the King during his battles, not only by being present themselves, fully equipped, but also by bringing along vassals, men who helped in the fighting. This practice was fairly universal in those days and many a knight came home from the Holy Wars totally impoverished. Nevertheless, they, too, had stewards, bailiffs or reeves who administered their lands, depending on the size of the estate involved. The people who worked on them could be villeins, small holders, or customary tenants. They held their lands by the custom of the manor. In early times, they could not move away from the estate without the lord's permission, and they had only his court to appeal to about their tenure.

They may have worked solely for their lord, who then provided for their needs, housing, clothing and feeding them. On the other hand, they may have held tenements, pieces of land which they tended for their own benefit, paying the lord with labour on his land as well as with produce from theirs. Later, both these kinds of obligations were replaced by cash payments. All this was very involved, needing much administration and settling of disputes; so the Lord of the Manor was not only entitled, but obliged, to hold court. During the court sessions, the Manorial Records were written up. From 1733, this had to be done in English, as in Cromwell's times. There were several types of sessions, dealing with different matters: the survey of lands; buildings; their value; their use and maintenance; and the rentals, for which there were lists of tenants with the amounts of rent. All this led to very involved accounts.

The records are written up on parchment, membranes made from animal skins, which were attached one to the other to literally form rolls; hence the name Manorial Rolls. The third part concerned the disputes and was known as the Manorial Court or later Court Baronial. The steward became more and more versed in the law, but each manor had its own rules, all based on precedence. There was a jury of 12 men chosen from the tenants, and all free men were obliged to attend a fixed number of sessions during the year. As time progressed, their names also appeared in the rolls: along with defaulters; or as tenants who wanted to surrender their holdings; or as people who had offended, perhaps by taking bracken illicitly from the woods, or having been found drunk; or as those who simply wanted to sublet their land. A fine had then much more the meaning of a payment fixed by agreement. For instance, if someone wished to brew ale for sale, he would make a regular annual payment, not for actual breaches of the assizes but, in effect, for licence to brew without risk of penalty for any breach that might occur.

Few of the early documents have survived and they varied greatly from manor to manor and over time. Manors were inherited, and might be joined with other lands. The Lord of the Manor might have forfeited his lands to the King for many reasons. The possibilities for variation would take books to describe. Once a manor had lost its last copyhold tenant, it could no longer hold a Court Baronial. Neither copyhold nor the Manor Court could be established after the early middle ages.

If the rolls have survived, they may be in private hands, local record offices, University Libraries, PRO Chancery Lane, the British Library of the British Museum in London, and elsewhere. Those of St Paul's Cathedral are in the Guildhall Library, London.

It is advisable to search first in the nearest record office. The librarian is often aware of the location of the rolls of the manors in the vicinity. Local libraries, antiquaries and history societies generally also know to which manor specific lands belonged. Once this has been established (keeping well in mind that the parish boundaries had nothing to do with the extent of the manorial lands), and the rolls cannot be found, then one can write with an SAE to the Royal Commission on Historic Manuscripts, Quality House, Quality Court, Chancery Lane, London WC2A 1HP. This institution holds no records whatsoever, but has an index on where to find historic manuscripts, such as Manorial Rolls.

A book containing much about the historic background, and also giving lists for further reading, is the fifth publication of the British Record Association, *Manorial Records*, by P D A Harvey, Professor of Medieval History at the University of Durham.

A booklet entitled, *Manorial Records*, was written by a genealogist, Mr P. Palgrave-Moore.

COURT OF QUARTER SESSIONS

First established in the 14th century, these county courts were held by justices of the peace, and presided over by the sheriff or his deputy. Their duties and roles changed over the centuries. In more recent times, they were the highest court of settlement disputes between 1740 and 1820.

Records have been in English since 1733, as they were during Cromwell's time. They fall into several groups: minute books; order books with formal records; and indictment books which deal with law suits and others. A few are in the PRO Chancery Lane, while most that have survived are in the corresponding CROs. They can give much biographical information about people. Details can be found in the guide, *Quarter Session Records* by J S W. Gibson.

TAX RECORDS AND ELECTORAL ROLLS

Throughout history, some taxes have been closely linked to the right to vote. 'Poll Taxes' were head taxes, and poll books listed the voters. Some of the early English poll books not only list those who were entitled to vote, but also those for whom they voted.

To this day, in Australia, the local council is elected by its rate-payers, and electoral rolls are kept.

Other electoral lists are regularly updated by the Electoral Office for each State, in the capital city. They and the major FHS libraries are likely to hold older lists, often on microfiche. In the SAGHS, Adelaide, you will find, on microfiche, the records for South Australia, for the House of Representatives and the Legislative Council, which corresponds to the Upper House or Senate. They cover the years 1884-1913, but the range is incomplete. In addition they have the electoral rolls for 1982, 1988, 1990, 1991, 1992 and 1993. The early ones are by divisions, while the modern ones list alphabetically the entire roll of voters for the state.

English citizens vote only for the members of the councils and the House of Representatives. Entry to the House of Lords is inherited or is conferred upon a person, who can only present himself for election (in the Lower House), by relinquishing his title. Lord Hume is an example of this. In Australia, members of the Upper house are also voted in by the electorate, which was limited until the 1960s, to owners of land. It has only since then included all ratepayers, and, latterly, all Australian citizens of age.

These electoral records can help trace the movements of a person, once he or she is identified.

Some of the earlier taxes and 'fines' in England are described under Manorial Records.

The Tithe was a church tax for one tenth of the income, and, as it was not imposed by parliament, may be described as illegal; but was paid nevertheless. It is said to have died out by 1832, but there is some evidence of payments in the 1840s. The tithe schedules would have been kept in the parish chest, and, if they have survived, are most likely to be in the CRO, along with the land tax records. These started in 1692 and are grouped by year.

Between 1694 and 1868, the right to vote was based mainly on the ownership of freehold land (except in boroughs). If the owner lived outside the parish, the poll books will give the address.

The poll books of freemen of cities and boroughs (mentioned under 'Education and Occupations') may have been printed and would give the names of those who voted in parliamentary elections. In London, they are likely to give the trade and the company of each person listed.

After 1832, electoral registers were printed.

There are several publications that can assist in the location of these records.

- Handlist of British Parliamentary Poll Books by J. Sims.

- Catalogue of Directories and Poll Books in the Possession of the Society of Genealogists by L. W. L. Edwards.

  In addition, there are four Gibson Guides:

- Land and Window Assessments.

- Poll Books c. 1696-1872.

- Electoral Registers since 1832 and Burgess Rolls.

- Hearth tax returns, other later Stuart Tax lists and the Association Oath Rolls.

EDUCATION AND OCCUPATIONS

SCHOOLS

School Admission Indexes, if they survive, are of limited value, as they often give only the name of the student, the date of admission and the date of leaving. However, there are some which also give details of previous schooling, if any, and the name and residence of the father, although rarely his occupation. When searching in South Australia, one may be lucky to find the pupil in the School Admission Index, in the SAGHS. The index was compiled from school records.

The name of the school can be found in the area directory, and the register may be in the school if it is still in existence, it or might have been deposited in the local library or record office. Other schools, including some English public (fee-paying) schools, have published records, and these can be found in libraries, in private collections or in second-hand bookshops. Some of these give information about those old scholars who maintained contact with the school during their later lives.

UNIVERSITIES

Most old, established universities publish registers, and these may be found in large libraries. For instance, 'Alumni Oxoniensis' (Oxford, up to 1892) and 'Alumni Cantabrigiensis' (Cambridge, up to 1900) can be found in Adelaide in the Barr-Smith Library of the University of Adelaide, as well as in the Flinders University Library.

Colin Chapman has recently published a book called *The Growth of British Education and its Records.*

APPRENTICES

If there was a contract of a formal training, which needed registration, then it may be traced, although the value of the search is limited.

Indentures made by the parish on behalf of the children of their poor were generally kept in the parish chest, and, where they survived, could now be in the local library or CRO.

However, between 1710 and 1804, formal training involving indentures called for a stamp duty to be paid. This practice led, in turn, to the compiling of records covering the British Isles, and they are now kept in the PRO Kew.

DIRECTORIES

Many have trade sections and lists of professionals. These can establish the presence of persons and their movements over the years.

Professional associations sometimes publish lists of their members, giving varying information.

Trade union records may assist you to follow the movements of an employee from firm to firm. In England, they should go sufficiently far back to permit the linking up with census returns, which give much more information.

Licences are required for a great number of occupations. These are issued by a licensing court, which was previously presided over by the Magistrate at Quarter Sessions. The court records give no information on the family, but simply show where the person was licensed and indicate the period of time for which the business was licensed.

In England, since the middle of the 16th century, publicans, drovers, dealers in corn, and other tradesmen needed licences, which were recorded by the clerk of the peace, who showed at the Quarter Sessions that all the fees had been paid. The book *Quarter Session Records* by J. S. W. Gibson has already been mentioned.

FREEMEN OF CITIES AND BOROUGHS

These had originally acquired their positions through apprenticeships. They were enrolled with the local authorities and were controlled by them. This gave them the right to trade there, and to vote in parliamentary elections.

The freedom could then be inherited and a London professional may, today, tell proudly of holding the tenth burgess ticket. It will have been passed on from the middle of the 18th century to this day. Sometimes even through sons-in-law, because their wives were direct heirs. The inheritance entitles him to be recognised as a member of the 10th generation of the Freemen of Glasgow. Here is an excellent example of a 'link document'.

If guilds and companies of cities survive, they can give similar information.

THE LONDON LIVERY COMPANIES

Their records are in the Guild Hall, London and must be consulted if an elusive ancestor has worked in this capital. They often give information regarding the origins of a person. Here, *My Ancestor was a Migrant,* by A. J. Camp, gives a list of further sources. An article, 'The City of London Freedom Register', by M. T. Medlycott, in the Genealogist's Magazine, Vol. 19, pages 45 - 47 and 141 - 2, would be of assistance. Both could well be on the shelves of your FHS library.

A great number of records concerning government employees, trades and professions, as well as armed forces, in England, are mentioned in *My Ancestor was a Migrant*. In it, leads to further research are given. Its author published recently the second edition entitled *My Ancestor Moved in England and Wales.*

THE ARMED FORCES

AUSTRALIA

- Air Forces - The Secretary, Department of Air, Canberra, ACT, 2601.

- Army records - ask for Service Number at the

  Australian War Memorial, Canberra ACT 2601 (for WWI records);

  then write, giving that number to

  Central Army Records Office, Box 1932 R GPO, Melbourne, VIC, 3001 (for WWII records).

- Navy records - The Secretary, Department of the Navy, Canberra, ACT, 2601.

H M BRITISH ARMED FORCES

The search of their records is a specialised field.

In general terms, the Ministry of Defence, Hayes, Middlesex, UB3 1RF, holds army records up to about 75 years. For the years before that, they can be found in PRO Kew. The earliest information, mostly concerning militia records, particularly between 1757 and 1812, and muster rolls for Yeomanry and Volunteer Corps after 1804, are likely to be found in the CRO of the area. Some militia lists are in print and as such, are more like a male census, as all men had to register - generally between 17 and 55 years of age - giving, among other things, marital status. Many have appeared in printed form, Jeremy Gibson and Sir Mervyn Medlycott wrote a guide *Militia Lists and Musters 1757 - 1876.*

Further leads can also be found in a series of articles by T. Wood in FTM of January 1989 (Vol 5), page 6; February, page 6; March, page 23.

One can find interesting background information in the most unexpected places. I found in *This England,* a Journal published in Cheltenham (Glos. England), articles on specific regiments, such as the Buffs (Winter 1982), Durham Light Infantry (Autumn 1983), the Dorset Regiments (Winter 1983), and the North Staffordshire Regiment (Spring 1984).

The records of the Royal Navy are at least as complex and varied. The library of the National Maritime Museum, Greenwich is vast and well worth a visit when in London.

The Ministry of Defence holds more recent records. Earlier ones may be found in the PRO Kew, which has published an eight page (A4) information pamphlet *Admiralty Records as Sources for Biography and Genealogy*. Apart from the above - mentioned sources, the FTM of September 1988 (Vol. 4) gives a long list of references on page 20.

MILITARY AND NAVAL RECORDS IN THE USA.

The best sources are the records of applications for pensions, whose issue began in 1790. Confederate veterans were not pensioned by the Federal Government, but by the States from which they began their service. Pension officials of these states usually have these records.

The papers of non-confederate veterans before WWI are in the National Archives. None before 1800 have survived. The catalogue of the LDS Church should be consulted, because microfilms of these records have been made by them since 1974. Most US libraries and record offices should be able to provide the General Services Administration form 6751, which should be completed and forwarded ,without remittance, to the Military Service Records (NNCC), National Archives (GSA), Washington DC 20408.

NONCONFORMISTS

There are some historical facts helpful to beginners investigating whether their ancestors may have been nonconformists, and wondering whether they should search those records.

The Roman Catholic Church was the Christian church in England until Henry VIII declared himself head of the Church of England in 1534.

The Lutheran Church (Germany), founded on 31.10.1517, was then the only well-established protestant church. Its adherents, particularly in South Australia, are likely to trace their ancestors back to Germany, most commonly Prussia.

Closely related to them are the Calvinists (France and Switzerland). The Huguenots are well known for having emigrated from France for religious reasons as from the 16th century. There is a Huguenot and Walloon Gazette Association, belonging to the FFHS. Most Huguenots entered England through the East End of London (look for *Cockney Ancestors* - the journal of the East-London FHS – on your FHS library shelves), to radiate to the Home Counties, and particularly to East Anglia. There were, however, a substantial number who entered through the South West coast, mostly from Bristol, through Cornwall to Devon. *Huguenot Ancestry* was written by N. Currer-Briggs and R. Gambier.

In England, the Church of England was not happily accepted by all. The history books will tell you much about the ups and downs of the Catholic Church – banned, reinstated and tolerated, all at different times. No wonder that registers, if kept at all, are difficult to find. People were afraid not only for their own lives but also for their loved ones. The priests' holes in contemporary castles and manors give evidence of the danger to them. Religious beliefs forced them to adhere to the rites of the Catholic Church, which demanded the ministry of a priest, yet raids were always a possibility, endangering all. So, ingenious devices allowed the priests to disappear behind walls, a little like the way that modern bookshelves can hide bars. This is an extreme case, but it has to be remembered that all nonconformists, called 'Dissenters', had similar fears; so one cannot be surprised at the scarcity of records made and kept.

There are two London-based groups belonging to the FFHS. They are the 'Catholic Record Society' and the 'English Catholic Ancestor'. However, if the parish is known and still exists, searches should begin there.

During the reign of Elizabeth I, the Church of England was the only recognised religious authority. The rites at that time were deemed by many as 'too popish', so many people were not happy – yet again. They formed 'sects', calling themselves Baptists, Congregationalists, Independents, Presbyterians, or Unitarians. They faced the same problems as the Catholics, and did, like them, survive to modern times.

The Methodists are in a class of their own, often known as the Wesleyan Church, after their founder, John Wesley. They originated in the second half of the 18th century.

The Moravians were founded in London and Oxford in the 1720s, the Wesley brothers being early members. Their records may be with local congregations, in the PRO Chancery Lane (from 1740 only), or at the Moravian Church House, Muswell Hill, London.

As dissidents were persecuted at times, it is more than understandable that they pretended to be Church of England parishioners, particularly when they wanted to marry legally. Some attended services, at least often enough to prevent their being reported to the authorities as not being true believers. Another problem faced , by them, was that of burial, as they had no cemeteries. (Private ones appeared mostly about the middle of the 19th century.) So, here again, nonconformists had often no choice but to go to the Church of England parish church. This fact makes it easier for the family historian to find at least some records. For a few years after 1696, Church of England ministers were obliged to register baptisms of nonconformists.

Lists of private burial grounds can be found in the appropriate

CRO, British Museum and SoG, London.

When you consistently see marriages by licence within a family, you should immediately think of nonconformists. Equally, one needs to acknowledge that, particularly in the early 1800s, ancestors were quite likely to change their loyalties to the church, even more than once. The word 'chapel' instead of 'church' is a firm indicator of nonconformists.

Between 1754 and 1837, only Quakers and Jews were allowed to marry legally according to their own rites. All others had to marry in the Church of England for the ceremony to be legal. Indeed some nonconformists used the Church of England for the rest of the 19th century for marriages.

Quaker records are very valuable, as they often give much information of interest, even if they do not have the formal birth-marriage and death registers of the Church of England. They have records in the Society of Friends Library, Friends House, Euston Road, London NW1 2BJ, but many of their records may also be in the CRO or PRO. The booklet,'*My Ancestors were Quakers,* by E. Milligan and M. J. Thomas, may prove helpful here.

Jewish records should be first searched locally – some FHS hold relevant work, done by their members, which needs to be asked for specifically, as it is not always on the open shelves. The Jewish Museum, Woburn House, Upper Worburn Place, London WC1, may be of help. The SoG has published a booklet by Michael Gandy *My ancestor was Jewish.*

On the whole, records of nonconformists may be in the PRO Chancery Lane, the relevant CRO, or elsewhere.

If you live in the Manchester area, you may wish to visit the John Ryland Library in Deansgate, Manchester, M13 9PL, which holds some nonconformist registers. The local FHS there has produced and printed an index, in book form, of all the parish nonconformist registers in the Manchester Local History Library. It covers virtually the whole of Lancashire.

This is another example of the large variety of research aids which are produced continuously by volunteers of FHSs, and emphasises why it is so beneficial to find out what is available in the area searched.

Understanding the History and Records of Non-Conformity by Patrick Palgrave-Moore is the beginner's 'reader', whilst the National Index of Parish Registers Series, Vol 2, *Sources of Non-conformists Genealogy and Family History*, and Vol 3, *Sources for Roman Catholic and Jewish Genealogy and Family History*, by Don Steel, are for the advanced searcher. The last two are published by Phillimore and Co. and can be purchased from them or through the SoG, London.

The paragraph on Church Record Keepers at the end of the chapter on Births-Deaths-Marriages deals with the USA.

EVALUATING CONFLICTING EVIDENCE

When you are establishing a family tree, there is bound to be some conflicting evidence.

For this reason, it is so very important from the beginning to note, very precisely, not only the information found including its source, the date and place where it was found, the name of the informant at the time of the event, as well as the finder. These details may help in later verification.

The birth of an ancestor occurs only once, as does the death. The same is usually true for the marriage of two people. However, I have come across one instance, where the same couple's marriage was registered twice in the indexes at St Catherine's House, in the same quarter and in the same district, but with different references. I suspect that they married at the Registrar's Office in a civil ceremony and then at church. This is the normal procedure in other countries. I have heard of others having come across similar cases.

RECORDS COME IN THREE GROUPS

1. Private family documents, such as a Bible, contemporary diary, etc.

2. Public or official records (registrar office, parish register, army records, census returns, etc.)

3. Printed sources, which are generally derived from the above sources; e.g. IGI, Monumental Inscriptions, etc.

The information transmitted through registers is only as good as the knowledge (or otherwise) of the informant.

The best information stems from the persons themselves. Personal knowledge is valued evidence in a court of law, but even here there are exceptions.

ALL FAMILY LEGEND IS SUBJECT TO FALLIBILITY

Contemporary written records contain few errors, but errors are fairly common in family Bibles when they are inscribed years after the event. Look at the year of the Bible's edition in question and relate that to the early entries. Then compare the handwritings.

Original wills are more accurate than copies.

Despite the pitfalls, there are few errors in records, but nothing is guaranteed to be correct.

Some consider that, up to a point, what has been told by an older person, perhaps a grand-parent, is not hearsay, provided the informant had direct personal knowledge. If that is supported by other evidence, then I would accept this information, otherwise I would treat it as a strong lead only.

All this explains why cross-referencing is so very important.

Census entries are very helpful but contain the most errors of all records. Those of the armed forces are known to be incomplete in many instances.

Pension files in the U.S.A. are established under oath.

Family histories, even when printed, are the least trustworthy.

A letter containing a statement of the writer's personal knowledge is a document and, as such, is a primary source.

Errors can easily arise from misreading or misinterpreting even the most accurate contemporary entry, simply because the reader is unfamiliar with the handwriting of the person and/or the old script characteristic of the period. Here, the McLaughlin Guide, *Reading Old Handwriting,* can be of immense value. If another language is involved, the problems are compounded. In such cases, photocopies of microfilms of the originals are a great help, as they can be consulted easily, as the knowledge of the searcher increases.

CONFLICTING EVIDENCE can concern a number of details:

- name

- place
- date (age)
- relationship

These discrepancies must be resolved as soon as they are discovered.

This is not a waste of time because it prevents errors being made and nearly always brings further evidence to light.

Names can be changed during a lifetime, for instance, by deed poll, but also, particularly in the older days, through usage. For instance, a boy was baptised in England, in the early 19th century, John Gordon Tayler, Gordon being his mother's maiden name. He had an elder brother, called John Thomson Tayler, after his paternal grandmother, born Thomson. Both boys survived; so the family called the younger one William. He was researched by his Australian offspring as William Tayler, with no second name. His wife was also known. The record of their marriage was found in England, in the parish of the bride, by licence. Bonds and allegations were searched. The groom was given as William Gordon Tayler, and witness to the marriage was John Thomson Tayler. The final link to the family of William Tayler was found on a death certificate, on which William Gordon Tayler had reported the death of his younger brother, Richard.

All over, Church records are more accurate than State records, because children's births are often registered by the hospital and the parents change their minds after registration.

Dates and ages should never be accepted safely from memory. Places are more likely to be correct and the greatest value lies in establishing family relationships.

The most common fault is found in marriage certificates. For example, the bride or groom were under 21 years of age and the parents would not give their consent. They were registered, unless the parish priest knew better, as of age. The census of 1841 is, in particular, notorious for misleading ages, due, in part, to the fact that adults were to give their ages to the nearest round figure.

It is a well-known fact that, at the beginning of a war, under-age volunteers lie about their ages in order to be accepted. Apart from that, people tend to describe themselves as younger rather than older.

Descrepencies about places can have many explanations. For example, in more recent times, children are more likely to be born in hospitals chosen for medical reasons, and these can be quite a way from the normal place of residence of the parents. In the past, it was common for a wife to go home to her parents for the birth of her first child and stay until well after the christening.

Marriages were not always performed in the family parish, particularly when either groom or bride came from elsewhere.

Death could have occurred away from the usual residence or family burial ground, and the body was brought home. The result was that different places were recorded on the death certificate and burial entry.

Relationships can be the most difficult of all to establish, particularly when a family had children with identical names. This information generally indicates that the elder had died before the other was born. Here letters, diaries and Bibles become important, and can be the most helpful guides to decision-making.

In the middle of the 18th century, roughly coinciding with the emergence of the first dictionaries, a concerted effort was made by the clergy to standardise the spelling of surnames. If the family remained resident over this period in the same parish, this change will become apparent to the searcher through an examination of all the family names in the register of that parish. Sometimes, one can see how the spelling of an individual's name was altered at a particular date. However, further 'link documents' will be needed to establish that the references, either side of that date, actually apply to the same person.

HISTORY AND FAMILY EVENTS

When finding out data about one's ancestors, one sometimes wonders why they did certain things. When they moved, the cause was often economic or health related, and sometimes both. The industrial revolution caused people to move from the country into the cities, and the cottage industries, which had prevented the poor from starving when there was no work on the farms, collapsed. The entire fabric of society was in turmoil. Napoleon destabilised the whole of Europe, and the English were in constant fear of invasion. So if the details of an ancestor's wedding and a birth of a child are known but there is no further information after that, one might get a lead by checking the general history of the country at that time. For this purpose, make a date list of historical events on the left side of the page, and on the right side, catalogue all the dated events known about the ancestors.

Assume that he disappeared just after 1800, in the South of England: If it is then known that, at that time, there was a great fear of a Napoleonic invassion, it would be logical to investigate what was done in the country to counter it. The answer would be that the communities, particularly along the coastline, established, around 1803, 'Militia Lists', already mentioned under 'Armed Forces'. All men between 17 and 55 years of age were listed. These lists were not new. The 1757 Militia Act re-established militia regiments in England and Wales, and their records can, for the years between 1757 - 1831, be used a little like an early census, even though incomplete. These lists are becoming increasingly available, and can be consulted in libraries or bought from the local FHS. There is an excellent article on this in the Genealogist's Magazine (SoG London), Vol. 23, pages 55 - 59 (June 1989). The Gibson Guide mentioned earlier (page 107) leads to them. Much earlier lists can sometimes be found, as they were drawn up in times of need.

Perhaps the name of the ancestor cannot be found in any likely militia list, even though he was young and, as far as is known, healthy. He might have gone into the Navy. That can be checked out in the naval records. Although this process is simple if one is researching officers, it is labourious for other ratings. If he did not go voluntarily, but was forced by the notorious press gangs, this fact might also emerge in the records. Some people could be protected against these, such as seamen and fishermen (two only for small boats) and their records are at the PRO Kew (ADM 7). Besides this, there were units of local seamen and fishermen, exercising together, forming a kind of marine militia. There are records, with names, payments, dates, and even signatures (or marks) for the receipt of money, in the PRO Kew (ADM 28). Later, one might wonder if he had emigrated, if information about him had still not been found; then it might be useful to search shipping lists.

A clue to the ancestor's occupation may be used as a lead. For instance, immediately after the Napoleonic wars, inflation rose in England. At the same time, English merchants expanded their businesses, trying to find overseas outlets for British products, and establishing trading posts, also called 'factories'. Generally, as agents, they sent brothers or close kinsmen, who may then have died abroad, never returning home.

One can, of course, make one's own historic lists, adapting them to the places and circumstances in which the ancestors lived. Some history books have chronological tables, such as the well known *Short History of the World,* by H. G. Wells, and the much more recent, *The World, an illustrated History,* edited by G. Parker, which is a companion to the South Carolina Educational TV Series, 'The World'. It is sometimes amazing how much information there is in High School history text books.

TRAVELLING ANCESTORS

Many live under the impression that it is only in recent times that people have begun to move about and settle in their new location. This is not so.

Presently, there is a surprising number of people who are looking for quite close relatives. The plight of adopted children who feel a need to find their biological parents has come to the forefront in recent years, and special government agencies involved in adoption can help. Advertising may be of assistance, while the Red Cross and similar organisations provide service for 'missing persons', particularly after disasters such as wars.

The FTM had a special column of 'missing live persons', which has now been incorporated into 'Connections sought', and which combines information on living and dead persons who are being sought.

In Australia, searching is fairly simple, compared to other countries. Records are largely organised on a State basis, and a great deal of information can be found in the capital cities, where the majority of the population lives. There are electoral rolls, register offices, and very active FHSs, bearing various names. There is at least one in each State, and they often have, as in England, branches elsewhere. For instance, the SAGHS in Adelaide has branches in Kadina (Yorke Peninsula FH Group) and Loxton (Riverland FH Group). Millicent is the centre for the South East Family History Society. They are run by volunteers who give advice to those who do not know where to search next. They also have topic groups, which specialise in such tasks as searching for Cornish, Scottish, Irish or German ancestors. Apart from journals of member societies of the FFHS, and books by the hundreds if not thousands, they have card indexes as mentioned earlier, directories and an ever - increasing number of printed biographical indexes. These provide an excellent starting point if the search is for people in the 19th century, particularly in South and Western Australia. These biographical indexes do not claim to be complete, but to be based on actual documents, such as entries in registers, shipping lists and the like. Very often, one finds the name of the ship on which a migrant arrived, the country of origin, and sometimes even the county. Many hold microforms of their own State and also of others. These collections may not cover all years. For instance, in Adelaide, there can be found in indexes of births, baptism and/or deaths and marriages from church and/or civil registers for New South Wales (1788–1905), Queensland (1829–1914), Tasmania (1803–1899), Victoria (1837–1913 and some later ones), Western Australia (1841–1905) and much, much more. All are listed in the library guide that is given to every member.

Added to this, there are the State Reference Libraries, which hold much material, sometimes housed apart, as in the Mortlock Library in Adelaide.

The majority of people in Australia, who research ancestors who lived in other countries do so in Europe. They can undertake the task by travelling there, by making use of agents, or by contacting others like themselves who are interested in the same ancestors. Mutually interested searchers can carry out research for one another, or exchange information, often by letter.

Those who look in the United Kingdom should have a lead as to the county in which to search. They would have gleaned this from the shipping lists in the country of arrival, the death certificates of the migrant ancestors, biographical indexes, or other documents. Barring this, with a name that is not too common, dictionaries of British surnames could give an idea of the counties in which the name is likely to be found. The one of P. H. Reaney (1958) is generally considered to be the authority, but there are many others: G. F. Black (1946); J. R. Dolan (1972); P. Hanks and F. Hodges (Oxford 1988); and C. M. Matthew (1966). Others can be found on page 128. From there, the IGI could be searched for clues to be followed up.

The most likely situation arises when the parish has been found and the trail of the ancestor disappears yet again. The classic approach is then (if the IGI gives no leads) to search the neighbouring parishes in ever - increasing circles. People moved easily over 20 miles. If the occupation of the ancestor is known, then this should be considered in conjuction with historical events even if they are only of local importance. For instance, when the production in mines in Devon and Cornwall fell, many miners migrated to the North of England, often to the Sunderland area, but some also went to Canada and Australia. Moonta in South Australia received many such families. *My Ancestor Was a Migrant* by A. J. Camp, who is the Director of Research of the SoG in London, would be a valuable and easily used guide. Its second edition is called *My Ancestors Moved in England and Wales.*

Those who do not search in England, might find the book *Worldwide Family History* by Noel Currer-Briggs, of help.

THE ELUSIVE GENTLEMAN

These were fairly common in the days of the British Empire.

The reasons for leaving the United Kingdom were manifold and not necessarily linked to economy or health. In some quarters, the 'Grand Tour' was considered by some as an essential part of education and a way of finding climates preferable to the English mist. Then there was the soldier, the adventurer, and the family father who saw no future in the Motherland and obtained parish assistance to pay for transport to America or Australia. Some left, not of their own free will, such as exiles or convicts. Even the last category is fairly easy to trace, as the records were well kept and their movements documented. Yet great care must be exercised. I was given quite an unusual name and a time of arrival in Australia. I found straight away that a person of that name arrived in South Australia on the date indicated from the appropriate county of origin. I could find no further trace of him in this State, which matched the information that 'he had eventually settled in the Eastern States'. So I sent my findings to my correspondent in England. With polite thanks for my efforts, she sent me supplementary information about the person researched who had the same very unusual name, and had arrived on the same day, but in New South Wales, and on a different ship from India. He had been a colonel in an English Regiment there and had, for health reasons, sold his commission and had come, with his English wife, two children and the necessary servants, to buy a tract of land. He could be traced very easily from there on. In this case, no harm was done, as the right person had been found. It could, however, have happened, that this man could have been confused with the other one of the same name, if no other 'link documents' had been consulted.

SOME SOURCES OF POSSIBLE INFORMATION

Consular Returns hold birth, marriage and death entries reported to the British Consuls abroad and these are in St Catherine's House. They began in 1849. It must be remembered that an entry could only be made if the Consul was informed. Miscellaneous registers are also there. RG 43 at PRO Chancery Lane has already been mentioned (p. 37) as the Index of 'Miscellaneous Foreign Returns'. The PCC wills and Admons should be searched, as probate for those Britons who died abroad would have been most likely granted at that Court.

Consular Records, as distinct from the above, are in the Guildhall, London. It is important to read Geoff Yeo's *The British Overseas*, updated periodically, published by the Guildhall, London and available from its Bookshop. Relevant information may be there, such as confirmation of a suspicion that a child was baptised abroad, by a chaplain officiating at a British Embassy, in 1780. This book states that the first baptism recorded in the 'International Memoranda' was in 1788; thus a search would be unnecessary.

Documents of the Foreign Office are in the PRO Kew.

The above addresses apply only to searches related to foreign countries. When the place searched was a colony or part of the Commonwealth, the local registrar and/or government archives need to be approached.

Passenger Lists are in the PRO Kew. Obtain leaflet No. 7, *Emigrants*. The records come under a section of the Board of Trade: BT XX 'Outwards' (XX being Roman Numerals).

Passport registers are also in the PRO Kew. It needs to be remembered that the obligation, to have a passport to travel, dates from World War I. Therefore early entries are rare and do not cover all travellers (Foreign Office: FO 610 1795–1943). They are in chronological order and show intended destination.

India, Burma, Pakistan and Bangladesh Records, virtually complete 1698–1947, are in the India Office Library and Records, 197 Blackfairs Road, London SE1 8NG. If you cannot go there yourself, you will need to employ an agent.

There is an ever increasing number of specialists societies. For instance, if you do not belong to a FHS with a German Group but wish to research in Germany, then contact the Anglo - German FHS. In recent years, an Anglo - French Association has also been formed, as distinct from the Huguenot & Walloon Gazette Association. Expect to receive much printed matter, such as information about joining the Association and what is offered. So, a large self-addressed envelope is indicated and more than basic postage. In these situations, I generally send twice the basic postage and add the difference to my 'Thank you' letter, or further correspondence.

In general, you can always try to locate FHS or Genealogical Societies in the area you are searching in, using the GRD. An increasing number of societies provide research facilities for members who live far away and generally charge double the fees for non-members.

The British–Australian Heritage Society, PO Box 5, St Thomas' Centre, Ryde, Isle of Wight, was formed to assist family history researchers who are tracing ancestors between Australia or New Zealand and the United Kingdom or Ireland. They charge a joining and a membership fee.

The Genealogical Research Institute of New Zealand GRINZ (PO Box 36, 107 Moera, Lower Hutt, New Zealand 6330), produces yearbooks. The one for 1989 is largely linked to research in Scotland/New Zealand.

The Australian Joint Copying Project involves all Australian State Libraries and began in 1948, when the first reel was produced in the PRO, London. Now there are many millions of pages on over 9000 reels. They are available, through the State Libraries of Australia and New Zealand, and handbooks are available, giving information about what has been filmed.

Most of the records copied date from 1767–1945, although the full period includes records from 1580–1975. Most are from the PRO.

SOCIAL MOBILITY

Most people find that their ancestors came from a variety of walks of life. It has been said that people who trace their ancestors to the 16th century will most likely discover links to the aristocracy. One need not go as far back to find family mobility, up and down the social scale. Some people find it very tempting, when they see a famous name appearing on their tree, to assume that there must be a close relationship, even a direct ancestor. This might well be, but the link must be established carefully, before a claim can be made.

In the case of armorials, the College of Arms, Queen Victoria Street, London EC4V 4BT, is the only authority that can confirm the right of a person to heraldic bearings, as it is responsible for all English and Welsh heraldry, and for much of that of the Irish and of the Commonwealth. The origins of heraldic bearings date from the times when people needed to be identified as friend or foe during armed combat, and when their armour made it impossible to recognise the man within. The oldest shields have the simplest designs. As they were inherited by children with more than one entitlement, they became more involved: They followed a rigid pattern, when even brothers would have differing designs, distinguishing between the elder and the younger, and, particularly in the case of a royal father, indicating whether the son was born in or out of wedlock. Besides shields, there were seals, which were needed to authenticate documents. Heraldry is a fascinating subject on which many good books have been written, and at least some of them should be on the shelves of your FHS or local library, or available through inter-library loan.

A word of warning. Recently, I received a letter asking for information, in which I was given quite a bit of very interesting medieval information from a French armorial general. The person had tried to link information from the end of the last century to the medieval data, and commented; 'Instead of retracing step-by-step, I had a tendency to jump backwards too fast at the one time - disaster! What a total waste of time and money...' I believe that the intuition of that person may be quite correct. However, in taking such an approach, how could one possibly be certain that a particular individual was actually one's ancestor? You can, of course, argue, that one can never be absolutely sure of one's ancestry, no matter how carefully the research has been done.

There are those who take advantage of people's ignorance, and sell them beautiful armorials for a given name, irrespective of the 'customer's' entitlement to it. I have been proudly shown more than one beautifully produced volume in handsome bindings, gold stamped with a family name, and bought at great expense. Each contained an article on the possible origins of the name, as well as addresses of people of the same name – gleaned from telephone directories.

THE ORIGINS OF SURNAMES

Contemplating the surname 'Kent', researchers could come to quite logical conclusions about its origins. It might be assumed that the ancestors moved, probably in the last part of the 13th or early 14th century from Kent to somewhere else. Over time, they could have acquired their surname from a shortening of the phrase, 'who came from Kent'. This might, of course, have been the case, but one cannot know this with certainty. There are other possibilities. Try to pronounce 'Cant' as many ways that you can think of while imitating local dialects, and a John who says 'I can't' could well become a John Kent.

Between the learned, there are some disagreements about the origins of names. However, there is one thing for which they must be given credit: they know the archaic languages and therefore contribute valuable knowledge.

They also mostly agree that it is for only a few landed families, that surnames go back to the 11th century. Most people's surnames developed during the second half of the 13th century and later. A comparison between modern names and those found in medieval documents reveals surprisingly constant trends. It is claimed that 42% of names originate from localities, 30% are patronymic (e.g. son of William = Williamson), 17% are derived from occupations and 11% come from personal appearance or nickname.

Imagine a medieval village. There were four men called John. The villagers needed to distinguish between them and therefore imposed names upon them, irrespective of whether the Johns involved liked them or not. These names, which developed into surnames, were found to consist of as many as four words. Take that John whose reply to requests for help was very often 'I can't do it today, maybe tomorrow?' He became 'John who can't', and, dialect permitting, John Kent by the 18th century, when spelling became important. The next John was a smith, so there was no problem. The third John lived near a pool, so 'John near the pool' became eventually John Pool. The fourth John, whose father was also called John, became eventually Johnson.

If you count the Smiths in any telephone book, you could easily conclude that there must have been an incredible number of smithies in the 13th century, many more than the community would have needed or could have supported. However, then, at least in the west of Yorkshire, a smithy was any iron-working site, such as a blast furnace or a place where iron-ore was dug, Consider the number of men who might thus have been known as 'John across the smithy' and the number of families called Smith is easier to understand.

Many years ago, at a party, a lady unrelated to my family told me that her ancestors were celts. Their name, Lavers, originated from their being slaves at the Roman baths in England. I showed myself dutifully impressed, although with a little knowledge of genealogy and some thought, I knew that such a claim could not be supported. On the surface, it seemed to make sense, because lavare, in Latin, means to wash, as laver does in French, to this day. If Lavers was mentioned at all, in the many dictionaries of names I consulted, a variety of origins were given. There was Laverton, a place with larks, or, in old English and Celtic, a place that was in the rushes or where the irises grew. In the middle ages, it was said to be of Anglo–Norman–French origin and referred to a washer of wool or flax. It was also described as a Celtic river name of unknown meaning, which related to the Loire, and which had inspired the name Leicester. Here was another connection with France. A very knowledgeable French genealogist, who researches the origins of names as a hobby, recognised Lavers immediately as very old French. It meant washer of wool, which made the bearer of it the owner of sheep. There was also the nickname, Lavers, that had originated from an old word of Provence. The word was aver and it meant to have, to possess. It had developed, by fusing with the article, into l'aver, the nickname for a rich man. The son of Laver could be Lavers.

Thus all four categories – location, occupation, patronyme and nickname – have been traced as possible origins of a single modern name.

What seems to be the more likely cause for the appearance of surnames was not necessarily the increased number of people between whom one had to distinguish, but possibly the greater mobility of people as they moved away from the feudal landed system. People no longer worked for an overlord, who in turn had cared for them and protected them. (It was, after all, very much in his interest.) These people now needed support, which they found within their families, which were recognised with greater ease when sharing the same surname. This theory is supported when you notice how children stayed often with relatives as apprentices during the middle ages, and how merchants used brothers or close kinsmen to take charge of their establishments in other cities or abroad. It is really only in our modern times that the extended family tends to disappear.

What good is it then to look at dictionaries of surnames? The answer is that very often they provide clues about where to search next.

Some noted reference books on the subject are available:

- G. F. Black, Surnames of Scotland (1946). A new edition is now available (ISBN 1 874744 07 6).
- Dr Marshall's Genealogist's Guide (up to 1903).
- Major Whitmore's Genealogical Guide (follows above to 1953).
- G. B. Barrow, The Genealogist Guide (follows up to 1977).
- C. W. Bardsley, A Dictionary of English and Welsh Surnames.
- The Penguin Dictionary of Surnames.
- Patrick Hanks & Flavia Hodges, Dictionary of Surnames.
- P. H. Reaney, Origin of English Surnames, is considered by many to be the authority.
- Gordon Jarvie - Scottish Names (Chambers 1992).

Others can be found in the chapter 'travelling ancestors'. (p 120)

There is one book that needs a special mention, as it is somewhat controversial. It is called *The Norman People*, a directory for medieval research by H. S. King; It was published in London in 1874 and reprinted by the Genealogical Publishing Co, Baltimore in 1975. He used the London telephone directory as a base and selected from it names which he thought would be of Norman origin. Then he tried to link those names to others which he could find in medieval documents in Normandy. I gather that he wanted to establish that the Normans, who had come to England in 1066, had left offspring. Because of the constant movement of people between the two countries in the intervening time, this would require the establishment of lines of descent, which gives this book a value in establishing that a given name could possibly have a French origin. The very number of people involved may well validate the author's claim. On the other hand, critics are undoubtedly justified in questioning such publications, particularly those from the Victorian era, for the reliability of their claims.

TO TELL OR NOT TO TELL that is the question

When hitting difficulties and suspecting a 'skeleton in the cupboard', what should one do? This is a question of ethics, and some may think that it does not belong in a 'how-to-do, hands-on guide' I think that it does.

My family, and the one I married into, have a well-developed sense of humour. There was one after-dinner story going around in family circles (and in family circles only) that described a certain ancestor having sent off two lusty sons on tall ships to keep them away from a very pretty step-mother. I was able to put that story to rest. There was no step-mother. Their own mother died one year after their father, and it was clear that they must have been a devoted couple, when details of their lives emerged. There cannot have been any animosity between father and sons. There are Foreign Office documents in the PRO Kew, where all three signed statements about events which they wished to be enquired into, for the good of all concerned. In the end, it became clear that the sons just went out, possibly in a spirit of adventure, to see the world.

In the chapter on the IGI, I described my approach to the LDS Church in Salt Lake City. Here, I had a birthdate, and a place of christening (without a date) that I could not find. It was the 'end of the line'. I needed the baptismal entry in the parish register, to learn the names of the parents and so continue from there. I searched through all the IGI geographical divisions which I thought appropriate, and was grateful that the name was not too common. Eventually, I found an entry: the date was later than the birth date which I had: the place could have been misread by the chronologer of family events who was slightly younger than the man I was looking for. However, the IGI entry showed no parents and that meant that he was a foundling. I was baffled. I kept it all quietly to myself and thought it out. What were my options? Was I prepared to accept that I was really dealing with a foundling? What would be the reaction of his elderly descendants, now in their eighties? I looked at what I knew of the man. In his time, no foundling could have achieved what he did. Was there a cover-up? Could he have done it? All his children had 'married well', one into the French aristocracy, who at that time were more aware of bloodlines than anyone else. They would have known if there had been a cover-up. Or would they? And so my thoughts continued. Finally I took the plunge. I just had to know and would decide later what to do with the information. I was fortunate; it was the fault of a negligent record keeper who had given only the names of the babies who were baptised, over several years, seventy to the page. I discovered to my joy that there had been no cover-up.

In circumstances like these, the decision must be yours, and you have to ask yourself 'Can I face the truth?' If you cannot, stop searching. If you can, go ahead, but be careful in divulging the truth: it may not be palatable or it may upset others in the family. The elderly, in particular, are very vulnerable. One always has the option of putting all findings into an envelope labelled 'open after my death', and then giving it to someone in the younger generation whose common sense and integrity one trusts. This seems to be a responsible decision.

There is another, much more immediate, aspect to the question. Should one share, with others, the information, that has cost much in research time, thought, and sometimes considerable expense? There are some fundamental rules adhered to by the majority of those who research.

1. IF one makes it known that one researches a certain thing, THEN one must answer queries on this topic by others.

2. IF one answers such a query published in a journal and wants an answer, or writes to any one with a problem for help, THEN one must send an SAE or at the very least 2 IRCs.

3. Nobody can neglect to answer any request which is accompanied by an SAE or IRCs. IF there is no time and the request is of no interest, and/or an answer cannot be given because it is not known, THEN the position needs simply to be stated in the margin and the letter sent back to its

writer. But this should be a very last resort: the information given might become of interest later.

4. DO NOT send, in the first letter to a fellow searcher, pages and pages of family history, BUT give enough information to enable the correspondent to distinguish between two people of the same name.

I read of a rather sad story, where a person researching one ancestor approached another person, suspecting he held all the information wanted. For twelve years, he could not get an answer, in spite of repeated approaches. In the end, he discovered that his suspicions had been right.

There may be two sides to that story. To begin with, it seems incredible that anyone could be so selfish as to withhold information on common ancestors. However, there may be other considerations, I have heard of and seen too many examples of people who want all the information as a matter of course, but who will not make any attempt to give some in return.

On the other hand, there is the urge to tell about one's findings, when one is caught up by the thrill of the latest discovery, and what it may imply. It is sometimes wise to curb this urge if one wants to keep one's friends.

JOURNALS AND BOOKS

All through the text, the journals of FHSs have been mentioned. There is one other journal that is very useful to the family historians. It is *The Family Tree Magazine*, a monthly publication of 56, A4 sized pages. It is described as 'The British Magazine with the International Flavour,' that started in November 1984 as a 32 page bi-monthly journal. Its articles were chosen to be helpful (not only to the beginner), as well as interesting and informative. It was also to have some advertising. To this were added, over the years, many items for which a need was felt by the publishers: a computerised root seeker; a stamp exchange service between British, Canadian, New Zealand, South African and USA stamps; 'Reader's Interests' list similar to those of the FHSs; 'Connections Sought' and other small advertisements for readers; an IGI self-serve or postal print-out service; and a postal book service which accepts cheques or notes in Australian, Canadian, New Zealand and US dollars. The exchange rates are given each month on the contents page. The latest addition is a computer section, which takes the place of the quarterly Family Tree Computer Magazine. The address is

The Family Tree Magazine
61 Great Whyte
Ramsey, Huntingdon
Cambs PE17 1HL

The request for backnumbers has been so great, that only a few of the more recent numbers can still be purchased. However, all are now available on microfiche, and can be bought as individual issues or by volume. The disadvantage of needing a reader is compensated for by the ease of storage.

The Family History News and Digests, the magazine of the FFHS, published in spring and autumn of each year, is well worth perusing, when one in searching over a wide field or looking for inspiration. Amongst other things, there are lists of important articles published by the member FHS societies. These give enough information, to enable one to judge whether the articles themselves should be examined.

They should be on every FHS library bookshelf for examination and for sale on all FHS bookstalls.

You may discover on the shelves of your FHS most of the books mentioned throughout this text. However, you may find, very often, that those which are the most helpful are not for loan, or are in such demand that access is not always easy. Purchase may be possible through your FHS or the above service. There are also specialised bookshops in which to browse.

There is one book not mentioned so far, that is a very valuable guide to British ancestry research. It is *The Dictionary of Genealogy* by Terrick V. H. FitzHugh, published by Alpha Books.

Stuart Raymond is another Author of an increasing number of publications which are most helpful in finding specific source material.

CARE OF DOCUMENTS

The fact that so many medieval documents survive is due to the fact that they were written on parchments, which are membranes obtained from animal skins. They were rolled up, and stored in dark places in order to keep them in best condition. As long as they were safe from vermin, mould, etc, they are in prime condition today.

Records on paper made from linen (flax) are also quite durable, but as this was expensive, other materials such as rags, were used, right into this century. Soon this was not enough and all the common, cheaper paper was made from wood. The bleaching methods applied , in order to make it white, not only polluted the environment, but also made the paper shortlived. If you are fortunate to have books from the 19th century, the chances are that you have noticed their pages turning yellow, even pale brown. This is one form of oxidation, similar to slow combustion; it is a kind of self-destruction. It is said that no paper made during the last 100 years will outlast 100 years.

Plastic coverings seem to be an excellent way of protecting valuable papers, but only if the plastic is acid-free. Old photographs are particularly vulnerable. As a basic rule, to prolong the life of precious items, they should be stored in a dark, dry place, safe from vermin. Use acid-free wrappings, such as specially made papers and acid-free plastics, uncoated mylar or triacetate sleeves – anything of an neutral pH. It is often described as having 'archival quality'. The items are best stored in acid free-boxes, flat and not compressed. There are many books on their conservation, by such bodies as the Royal Photographic Society of Britain and by the American Association for State and Local History.

No PVC should be used. Some other plastics will break down and affect the ink. Some specialists suggest testing plastics by using a small length of thin copper wire. Heat it until it is red hot in a gas flame that is no longer green. Touch the plastic with the hot wire and put the wire back into the flame. If the flame turns green again, do NOT use the plastic. This is known as the Beilstein test. 'Archive safe' materials available from commercial outlets are the best.

Neither cardboard nor glue should be used in framing documents.

Do not forget to label all photographs on their backs (e.g. H W J with his grandsons, London, 1940).

IS THIS ALL?

No, it is not. This is only an introduction,with an inbuilt reading list, so that readers can be guided to appropriate sources. From these, they should be able to find new ones, that may be more suitable to the specific problem.

The use of tax records provides an example of this kind of process. Governments have not altered much through history: they always need more money. The Domesday Book can be seen as a register of the Inland Revenue or Tax Department. Governments have another thing in common: when forced to abolish one tax, they find another to take its place.

There was the 'Hearth Tax', that came into force in May 1662 and was abolished in 1689. Those who did not have to pay parish taxes (such as the poor), were exempt but still were registered along with the rest of the populace. Some lists for this tax are printed, even indexed. Times have not changed; people complained bitterly about that tax and its 'invasion of privacy', and the Government gave in. Instead, the window tax (1696) was introduced, with the same rules. However, the 'inspectors' could count the windows without entering the houses. There was, predictably, a response: all unnecessary windows were 'bricked up' and people called it the 'tax for light and air', neither of which is provided by any government. It was only in 1851 that this tax was finally abolished.

The records of the window tax can be found in the PRO Chancery Lane, under E181 (exchequer), and both tax records can be used as census returns for heads of households.

Go from there to the embroidered sampler of an x times great-grandmother; she might have produced it between the ages of 7 and 17. When looking at the stitches, one can get a clue to her date of birth.

The ancestral search is as individual as each of us. Biologists tell us that only identical twins are the same. A family tree is the same only for siblings, those who have the same parents.

Remember, every person has records. The questions are whether those records have survived and whether they will be found.

GOOD HUNTING!

APPENDIX I
CHAPMAN CODES OF COUNTRIES AND COUNTIES

COUNTRIES

Australia	AUS
Austria	OES
Belgium	BEL
Canada	CAN
Czechoslovakia	CS
Denmark	DEN
England	ENG
Finland	FIN
France	FRA
German Old Empire	GER
Greece	GR
Hungary	HU
Ireland (Eire)	IRL
Isle of Man	IOM
Italy	ITL
Netherlands	NL
New Zealand	NZ
Norway	NOR
Papua New Guinea	PNG
Poland	POL
Portugal	PT
Rep. South Africa	RSA
Roumania	RO
Scotland	SCT
Soviet Union (USSR)	SU
Spain	ESP
Sweden	SWE
Switzerland	CH
United Kingdom	UK
United States	USA
Wales	WLS
Yugoslavia	YU

AUSTRALIA (AUS)

Australian Capital Territory	ACT
New South Wales	NSW
Northern Territory	NT
Queensland	QLD
South Australia	SA
Tasmania	TAS
Victoria	VIC
Western Australia	WA

ENGLAND (ENG)

Bedfordshire	BDF
Berkshire	BRK
Buckinghamshire	BKM
Cambridgeshire	CAM
Cheshire	CHS
Cornwall	CON
Cumberland	CUL
Derbyshire	DBY
Devon	DEV
Dorset	DOR
Durham	DUR
Essex	ESS
Gloucestershire	GLS
Hampshire	HAM
Herefordshire	HEF
Hertfordshire	HRT
Huntingdonshire	HUN
Kent	KEN
Lancashire	LAN
Leicestershire	LEI
Lincolnshire	LIN
London	LND
Middlesex	MDX
Norfolk	NFK
Northamptonshire	NTH
Northumberland	NBL
Nottinghamshire	NTT
Oxfordshire	OXF
Rutland	RUT
Shropshire	SAL
Somerset	SOM
Staffordshire	STS
Suffolk	SFK
Surrey	SRY
Sussex	SSX
Warwickshire	WAR
Westmoreland	WES
Wiltshire	WIL
Worcestershire	WOR
Yorkshire	YKS
YKS East Riding	ERY
YKS North Riding	NRY
YKS West Riding	WRY

ISLANDS

Alderney	ALD
Channel Islands	CHI
Guernsey	GSY
Isle of Man	IOM
Jersey	JSY
Sark	SRK

IRELAND (IRL)

Antrim	ANT
Armagh	ARM
Carlow	CAR
Cavan	CAV
Clare	CLA
Cork	COR
Derry	DRY
Donegal	DON
Down	DOW
Dublin	DUB
Fermanagh	FER
Galway	GAL
Kerry	KER
Kildare	KID
Kilkenny	KIK
Leitrim	LET
Leix (Queens)	LEX
Limerick	LIM
Londonderry	LDY
Longford	LOG
Louth	LOU
Mayo	MAY
Meath	MEA
Monaghan	MOG
Offaly (Kings)	OFF
Roscommon	ROS
Sligo	SLI
Tipperary	TIP
Tyrone	TYR
Waterford	WAT
Westmeath	WEM
Wexford	WEX
Wicklow	WIC

SCOTLAND (SCT)

Aberdeen	ABD
Angus	ANS
Argyll	ARL
Ayr	AYR

SCOTLAND (SCT)

Banff	BAN
Berwick	BEW
Bute	BUT
Caithness	CAI
Clackmannon	CLK
Dumfries	DFS
Dunbarton	DNB
East Lothian	ELN
Fife	FIF
Inverness	INV
Kincardine	KCD
Kinross	KRS
Kirkcudbright	KKD
Lanark	LKS
Midlothian	MLN
Moray	MOR
Nairn	NAI
Orkney	OKI
Peebles	PEE
Perth	PER
Renfrew	RFW
Ross & Cromarty	ROC
Roxburgh	ROX
Selkirk	SEL
Shetland	SHI
Stirling	STI
Sutherland	SUT
West Lothian	WLN
Wigtown	WIG

WALES (WLS)

Anglesey	AGY
Brecknockshire	BRE
Caernarvon	CAE
Cardiganshire	CGN
Carmarthan	CMN
Denbighshire	DEN
Flintshire	FLN
Glamorgan	GLA
Merioneth	MER
Monmouthshire	MON
Montgomeryshire	MGY
Pembroke	PEM
Radnorshire	RAD

APPENDIX II
CODES EMPLOYED AT ST. CATHERINE'S HOUSE

ROMAN NUMERALS

1837-1851

I	London & Middlesex
II	London & Middlesex
III	London & Middlesex
IV	London & Surrey
V	Kent
VI	Beds., Berks., Bucks. & Herts.
VII	Hants & Sussex
VIII	Dorset, Hants. & Wilts
IX	Cornwall & Devon
X	Devon & Somerset
XI	Glos., Soms. & Warwicks
XII	Essex & Suffolk
XIII	Norfolk & Suffolk
XIV	Cambs., Hunts & Lincs.
XV	Leics., Northants., Notts & Rutland
XVI	Oxon., Staffs. & Warwicks
XVII	Staffordshire
XVIII	Glos., Salop., Staffs., Warwicks. & Worcs.
XIX	Cheshire, Derbys. & Flints
XX	Lancashire
XXI	Lancashire & Yorkshire
XXII	Yorkshire
XXIII	Yorkshire
XXIV	Durham & Yorkshire
XXV	Cumberland, Lancashire, Northumberland & Westmorland
XXVI	Brecknocks, Carmarthens., Glams., Herefords., Mons., Pembs., Randors. & Salop
XXVII	Anglesey, Caernarvons., Cardigans, Denbighs., Flints., Merioneths. & Montgomeryshire.

N.B. As the older volumes (above) are replaced, the Roman numerals are being replaced by Arabic.

ARABIC WITH SMALL LETTER

1852 - AUG 1946

1a	London & Middlesex
1b	London & Middlesex
1c	London & Middlesex
1d	London, Kent & Surrey
2a	Kent & Surrey
2b	Hants & Sussex
2c	Berks. & Hants
3a	Berks., Bucks., Herts., Middx. & Oxon
3b	Beds., Cambs., Hunts., Northants. & Suffolk
4a	Essex & Suffolk
4b	Norfolk
5a	Dorset & Wiltshire
5b	Devonshire
5c	Cornwall & Soms
6a	Glos. Herefords. & Salop.
6b	Staffs., Warwicks. & Worcs.
6c	Warwicks. & Worcestershire
6d	Warwickshire
7a	Leics., Lincs & Rutland
7b	Derbyshire & Notts.
8a	Cheshire
8b	Lancashire
8c	Lancashire
8d	Lancashire
8e	Lancashire
9a	Yorkshire
9b	Yorkshire
9c	Yorkshire
9d	Yorkshire
10a	Durham
10b	Cumberland, Northumberland & Westmorland
11a	Glamorgan., Monmouth. & Pembrokeshire
11b	Anglesey, Brecknocks., Denbighs., Flints., Montgomeryshire & Radnorshire

APPENDIX III

SOME ENGLISH COUNTY RECORD OFFICES

AVON	Bath Record Office: Guildhall, Hight Street, Bath, Avon, BA1 5AW
BEDFORDSHIRE	Bedfordshire R.O., County Hall, Cauldwell Street, Bedford MK42 9AP.
BERKSHIRE	Berkshire R.O., Shire Hall, Shinfield Park, Reading RG2 9XD
BUCKINGHAMSHIRE	Buckinghamshire R.O., County Hall, Walton Street, Aylesbury HP20 1UA.
CAMBRIDGESHIRE	Cambridgeshire R.O. Shire Hall, Castle Hill, Cambridge CB3 0AP.
CHESHIRE	Cheshire R.O. Duke Street, Chester CH1 1RL
	Chester City R.O., Town Hall, Chester CH1 2HJ
CORNWALL	Cornwall R.O., County Hall, Truro TR1 3AY
CUMBERLAND	Cumbria R.O., The Castle, Carlisle CA3 8UR
	Cumbria R.O., 140 Duke Street, Barrow-in-Furness LA14 1XW
	Cumbria R.O. Kendal County Office, Stricklandgate, Kendal, LA9 4RQ
DERBYSHIRE	Derbyshire R.O., Education Dept., County Offices, Matlock DE4 3AG
DEVON	Devon R.O. Castle Street, Exeter EX4 3PU
	West Devon R.O., 3 Clare Pl., Coxside, Plymouth PL4 0JW
	North Devon R.O. Tuly Street, Barnstaple EX32 7EJ
DORSET	Dorset R.O., County Hall, Bridport Road Dorchester DT1 1RP
DURHAM	Durham County R.O., County Hall, Durham DH1 5UL
	Cleveland Archives Dept., 6 Marton Road, Middlesborough TS1 1DB
ESSEX	Essex R.O., County Hall, Victoria Road South, Chelmsford CM1 1LX
	Essex R.O., Stanwell House, Stanwell Street, Colchester CO2 7DL
	Essex R.O., Library, Victoria Avenue, Southend-on-Sea SS2 6EX
GLOUCESTERSHIRE	Gloucestershire R.O., Clarence Row, Alvin Street, Gloucester GL1 3DW
	Bristol R.O., The Council House, College Green, Bristol BS1 5TL
HAMPSHIRE	Hampshire R.O., Sussex Street, Winchester SO23 8TH
	Isle of Wight County R.O., 26 Hillside, Newport PO30 2EB
	Portsmouth City R.O., 3 Museum Road, Portsmouth PO1 2LE

HAMPSHIRE	Southampton City R.O., Civic Centre, Southampton SO9 4XR
HEREFORDSHIRE	Hereford & Worcester R.O., County Hall, Spetchly Road, Worcester WR5 2NP
	Hereford R.O., The Old Barracks, Harold Street, Hereford HR1 2QX
HERTFORDSHIRE	Hertfordshire R.O., County Hall, Hertford SG13 8DE
HUNTINGDON	Cambridgeshire R.O., Grammar School Walk, Huntingdon PO18 6LF
KENT	Kent Archives Office, County Hall, Maidstone ME14 1XQ
	West Kent Archives Office, Central Library, The Drive, Sevenoaks
	Kent Archives Office, Library, 2 Grace Hill, Folkestone CT20 1HD
	Kent Archives Office, Library, Guildford Lawn, Ramsgate CT11 9AI
LANCASHIRE	Lancashire R.O., Bow Lane, Preston PR1 8ND
	Liverpool R.O., City Library, William Brown Street, Liverpool L3 8EW
	Merseyside Maritime Museum, Albert Dock, Liverpool L3 4AA
	Greater Manchester County R.O., 56 Marshall Street, New Cross, Manchester MA 5FU.
LEICESTER	Leicestershire R.O., 57 New Walk, Leicester LE1 7JB
LINCOLNSHIRE	Lincolnshire Archives, St Rumbold Street, Lincoln, LN2 5AB
	South Humberside, Area Archive Office, Town Hall Square, Grimsby DN31 1HX
LONDON	Greater London Record Office, 40 Northampton Road, London EC1R 0HB
	Corporation of LONDON Record Office, P.O. Box 270 Guildhall LONDON, EC2P 2EJ
	Guildhall Library (covers city) Aldermansbury London EC2P 2EJ
NORFOLK	Norfolk R.O., Central Library, Norwich NR2 1NJ
NORTHAMPTON	Northampton R.O., Wootoon Hall Park, Northampton, NN4 8BQ
NORTHUMBERLAND	Northumberland R.O., Melton Park, North Gosforth, Newcastle upon Tyne NE3 5QX
	Berwick upon Tweed R.O., Council Office Wallace Green, Berwick upon Tweed TD15 1ED
NOTTINGHAMSHIRE	Nottinghamshire R.O., County House, Castle Meadow Road, Nottingham NG2 1AG
OXFORDSHIRE	Oxfordshire R.O., County Hall, New Road, Oxford OX1 1ND
SHROPSHIRE	Shropshire R.O., Shirehall, Abbey Foregate, Shrewsbury SY2 6ND.

SOMERSET	Somerset R.O., Obridge Road, Taunton TA2 7PU Avon-Bath City R.O., Guildhall, High Street, Bath BA1 5AW
STAFFORDSHIRE	Staffordshire R.O., Eastgate Street, Stafford, ST16 2LZ Lichfield Joint R.O., Lichfield Library, The Friary, Lichfield WS13 6QG.
SUFFOLK	Suffolk R.O., Gatacre Road, Ipswich IP1 2LQ Suffolk R.O., Local Studies Library, 77 Raingate Street., Bury St Edmunds IP33 2AR Suffolk R.O., Lowestoft Branch, Clapham Road, Central Library, Lowestoft Suffolk NR32 1DR.
SURREY	Surrey R.O., County Hall, Penrhyn Road, Kingston upon Thames KT1 2DN
SUSSEX	East Sussex R.O. The Maltings, Castle Precincts, Lewes BN7 1YT West Sussex R.O., County Hall, Orchard Street, Chichester PO19 1RN
WARWICKSHIRE	Warwick County R.O., Priory Park, Cape Road, Warwick CV34 4JS West Midlands - Birmingham Archives, Chamberlain Square, Birmingham B3 3HQ
WESTMORLAND	Cumbria R.O., County Offices Stricklandgate Kendal LA9 4RQ
WILTSHIRE	Wiltshire R.O., County Hall, Trowbridge BA14 8JG
WORCESTER	Herefod and Worcester R.O., County Hall, Spetchley Road, Worcester WR5 2NP Worcester (St Helen's) R.O., Fish Street, Worcester WR1 2HW
YORKSHIRE	Borthwick Institute of Historical Research, University of York, St. Anthony's Hall Peasholme Green, York, YO1 2PW York City Archives, Art Gallery Buildings, Exhibition Square, York YO1 2EW Sheffield Archives, 52 Shoreham Street, Sheffield S1 4SP North Yorkshire County R.O., County Hall, Malpas Road, Northallerton DL7 8AD Yorkshire Archeological Society, Claremont, 23 Clarendon Road, Leeds LS2 9NZ West Yorkshire Archives, Chapeltown Road, Sheepscar Leeds LS7 3AP Kingston upon Hull City R.O., 79 Lowgate, Hull HU1 2AA Humberside County R.O., County Hall, Beverley HU17 9BA Rotherham Central Library, Archives and Local Studies Section, Walker Place, Rotherham S63 1JH Wakefield Libraries H Q Dept of Local Studies and Archives Balne Lane Wakefield WF2 ODQ

See Also	:	Record Offices: How to find them (Gibson Guide)
	:	In and around Record Repositories in Great Britain and Ireland (1992 edition) by Sean Cole and Rosemary Church would be valuable sources for more addresses. The Section 'Archives' of the GRD 1994 and entries in earlier editions give more addresses including other countries.

INDEX

Page numbers are given only once
although items may appear several times

Items and addresses are also found under countries.

NOTES

NOTES

NOTES

NOTES

NOTES

NOTES

NOTES

NOTES

NOTES

NOTES

NOTES